A PERSONAL GUIDE TO OFFSHORING IN INDIA

A PERSONAL GUIDE TO OFFSHORING IN INDIA

To order additional copies of this book, contact:
Xlibris Corporation
1-888-795-4274
www.Xlibris.com
Orders@Xlibris.com
21043

CONTENTS

SECTION FOUR 71

SECTION FIVE 113

SECTION SIX 155

SECTION SEVEN 171

SECTION EIGHT 191

ACKNOWLEDGEMENTS

With the writing of this book, I feel that I have landed . . . landed my most exhilarating purpose of connecting people around the world. My passion, however, may well have been like Thomas Gray's flower "born to blush unseen" had it not been for all of the following:

Stewart Lytle for planting the seed. Stewart, a product of Andover and Princeton, is a man of letters, but even more a man of ideas, and he is singularly responsible for getting me started and making me stay the course. Ashank Desai, Sudhakar Ram, and Ketan Mehta – the founders of Mastek/ Majesco – for nurturing the idea and allowing me company time and money to do justice to the book. Santanu Das, a colorful merchant marine/IT marketer, for toiling in the research weeds that can choke such a venture. Ted Fine, my guru for "training" the plant; Alan Hodel, the self effacing, superbly effective editor, for pruning it; Kaajal Shaikh and Vinod Kerkar for enthusiastically 'landscaping' our work; and our many customers and colleagues who sprinkled inputs, like water, to help the book grow.

While many contributors will remain unnamed, I would be remiss to not acknowledge Joe Cooper, Raju Oak, Vimla Verghese, Tapan Bose, Sanjay Mudnaney, Rajshekhar, Durga Prasad, Mita Rout, and Uma Nadkarni, who contributed ideas, stories and important details. Equally, the minds at McKinsey, Forrester, Gartner and the many other think tanks whose research and ideas have frankly given credence to our industry and this book.

The Preface and the Foreword are very special to me because they are written by people who know whereof they speak.

Gurcharan Das had long been a role model for me – a successful packaged goods marketer who rose to run businesses and then to his true calling: writing. He has empathy and has lived the worlds we are trying to bridge with this book. It is an honor to have a celebrated author and authority like him endorse the idea and contribute to readers' understanding of offshoring in India. While Gurcharan makes the business case, Ted Fine, a brilliant technologist and former Citibank International CIO, does likewise for technology. Ted architects solutions like Mozart wrote music. He sees things before others do. I am grateful he saw the potential of this book and helped us frame it right.

Going back in time to the many that help make the man. My father, Brigadier General O.P. Vohra, for believing in me, regardless. My mother, Kamla, and soul mate, Ritika, for loving, but challenging me relentlessly. Ritika's family for globalizing me, literally. My sisters, Renuka and Neelam, and the Christian Brothers of St. Columba's High School for teaching me to communicate with sensitivity. And, now to my daughters, Taarini and Shivani, who inspire me, unfailingly.

Thank you all. I hope I have done you proud.

**TO INDIA, WHICH PREPARED ME FOR THE WORLD,
AND TO AMERICA, WHICH OPENED THE WORLD...**

SECTION ONE

PREFACE

BY GURCHARAN DAS

Why are the best American companies more nimble and innovative than their European counterparts? It is their willingness to try something new and, if that doesn't work, turn around and try something else. (Of course, if the first idea works, the American company implements it throughout the organization with a sense of urgency.)

This simple fact explains why more than 200 American *Fortune 500* companies are saving hundreds of millions of dollars while becoming more competitive by outsourcing services to India – especially in the information technology sector. What began as a small experiment by a few companies in the mid-1990s is turning into a tidal wave as more and more companies realize they must leverage offshore outsourcing to remain competitive.

Outsourcing is the common sense idea that you don't do something yourself if someone else can do it for you better and cheaper. Many American companies have implemented this simple idea, gaining enormous financial rewards as a result. Offshore outsourcing extends this approach overseas where cheaper, better – and more reliable – vendors have emerged.

Offshore outsourcing of manufacturing became widespread in the 1980s. Services outsourcing was the inevitable result of the global telecommunications revolution and phenomenal growth of the Internet in the 1990s.

Two global trends converged in the 1990s to bring about the revolution in outsourcing services to offshore vendors, providing huge benefits to both developed Western countries, like the United States, and poorer countries with intellectual capital, like India. The first trend is a liberal revolution that has swept the globe in the past decade after the collapse of Communism; it has opened economies that were isolated for 50 years and integrated them into a single global economy. India's economic reforms are part of this trend and, since 1991, India has been de-regulating, dismantling bureaucratic controls over economic activity, creating competitive markets and releasing the long suppressed energies of its people.

As a result, the mindset of the nation has changed rapidly, as documented in my book, *India Unbound.*[1] Results of India's economic reforms are dramatic: high rates of economic growth, visible prosperity, and rapid creation of a middle class that is an increasingly vibrant market for the products of America and the developed West. With the end of the Cold War, the two largest democracies in the world – the U.S. and India – also have come closer together politically.

The second global trend is the transformation of the world's economy from a manufacturing to a knowledge-based economy. This has played, oddly enough, to the advantage of a country like India, which has an almost obsessive reverence for knowledge. For example, in 1995 six Indians went to college for every Chinese who went to college. The Indian Institutes of Technology (IITs) routinely produce world-class engineers, some of whom helped create the technology miracle in Silicon Valley.

Getting into one of the fiercely competitive Institutes is more difficult than getting into Harvard. Only 3,500 students are accepted from the 180,000 who apply each year – an acceptance rate of 2 percent compared to 10 percent for Harvard.

Indian's respect for knowledge dates back thousands of years. Mankind's first book, *The Rig Veda*, was written in the second millennium B.C. in northwest India. The Brahmin scholar has always been at the top of the caste hierarchy, and he has historically inculcated respect for conceptual knowledge deep into Indian society. For thousands of years Indians have produced texts in philosophy, statecraft, art, and reli-

---

[1] Publisher: Knopf, (February 13, 2001)

gion, wrestling with abstract concepts in mathematics and astronomy. For example, Indians invented the concept of "zero," giving rise to the decimal system, which reached the West through Arabic scholars.

India's information technology services boom can only be understood against this background. During the decade of the 1990s software exports grew at a blistering 60 percent a year, and the annual revenues of the 500 largest Indian IT companies passed $10 billion in 2003. Even in the midst of a global slowdown in 2001-2003, Indian IT companies continued to grow in excess of 25 percent, due to American companies' insatiable appetite to cut costs during the slowdown.

In addition, all the major software companies in the world have created a development center in India, including IBM, Microsoft, HP, SAP, Cisco, and Oracle. A.T. Kearney projects that the financial sector alone could save $30 billion in costs through offshore outsourcing. Some 82 percent of American companies rank India as the destination of choice for outsourcing software and R&D work. The value of G.E.'s outsourcing work to India alone exceeds $500 million. McKinsey projects that India's software exports will surpass $50 billion annually – and IT enabled services $17 billion annually – by 2008.

Many scholars predicted that developed countries would specialize in knowledge industries while poor, less-developed countries were relegated to lower-wage, lower-skill industries. At least, this was the theory, but someone forgot to tell Mumbai and Bangalore . . . and Hyderabad, Chennai, Gurgaon, Pune, and the other high tech cities in India. Everyday, yet another American *Fortune 500* company decides to outsource its IT services to India. Clients in America e-mail their needs before they leave the office and, while they sleep, Indian engineers work to solve their problems. Often, by the next morning, as the Americans bring their coffee mugs to their desks, they have their answers as they log on.

There are deep anxieties about globalization all over the world. The prospect of job losses in local communities in the West as a result of outsourcing services offshore is real. It is the same sentiment that Indian workers have been feeling about their jobs when tariff barriers began crumbling in India after the economic reforms. But the reality is that globalization is irreversible; if anything, it is going to accelerate in the 21st century.

It is the responsibility of corporate executives and political states-men to reassure ordinary citizens that, in the long run, free trade is good for everyone, even though it may appear to cause some pain to some in the short run. In reality, the Bureau of Labor Statistics projects a coming labor shortage of around 10 million jobs in the U.S., many in the high-skill areas of information technology services. This gap will logically have to be made up at least partially through offshore outsourcing of services.

Similar fears of job losses were expressed in America in the 1990s when the North American Free Trade Association (NAFTA) was being debated. It took a strong public-private partnership of the American ad-ministration and the corporate sector to succeed in reassuring American workers that although some American jobs would be exported to Mexico and Canada, many more higher paying jobs would in the end be created in America.

And they were right. Multiple studies have since shown that every-one gained with NAFTA – Mexico, Canada, and the U.S. As a matter of fact, the last five years of the 1990s saw an unprecedented drop in the U.S. unemployment rate. Similarly, it will take the same courageous leader-ship to convince people around the world that open societies, free trade, and multiplying connections to the global economy are the pathways to lasting prosperity and the democratic comity of all nations.

Some Indians worry that the Chinese will soon catch up in informa-tion technology and their present dominance may erode in the future. I personally do not believe this will happen soon because of the natural and historical advantage that Indians enjoy with the English language. The 200-year-old historic connection with Britain has resulted in giving about 60 million Indians today the facility to converse in English with ease (and another 150 million aspirants to struggle with English with varying levels of success).

Linguistic experts also confirm that Indians find it easier to learn English than do the Chinese because the Indian languages are part of the Indo-European family, sharing a similar structure and grammar. The Chi-nese – much like the Japanese – find learning English a more difficult task, in part because the languages of East Asia are tonal and have thou-sands of characters. The same word in Mandarin can have many meanings depending on the tone in which it is spoken. Hence, Chinese have difficulty coping with English grammar and pronunciation. India's success in the global services economy lies in part with the ease with which Indians converse in English, and this competitive advantage is not likely to disappear easily.

The world in the 21st century will see the relentless push of the global economy and communications, supported avidly by a rapidly growing middle class in countries like India and China. We will see the irresistible spread of competitive markets and social democracy. With the 9/11 attacks there has been a rise in fundamentalism and growing consciousness of religious identity in the world. Despite this, I believe the primary preoccupations of the world's people will be with a rising standard of living, with social mobility, and with the peaceful pursuit of middle-class values and culture.

Just as the Chinese think they may have found a way to become the world's shop floor, so do many Indians think that they could become its back office. As a result, they believe that they may have finally found the engines that could one day transform their countries, in the same way that textile exports from the mills of Lancashire transformed Britain in the 19th century and the railways transformed America. With the rise of the Chinese and Indian economies the world faces the very real prospect of conquering the pervasive poverty that has characterized the lives of the majority of its people. We have, thus, good reason to expect that the lives of increasing numbers of people in the 21st century will be freer, more humane, and more prosperous than their parents' and grandparents' lives. Never before in recorded history have so many people been in a position to rise from poverty so quickly.

Good managers everywhere are confident and instinctively believe in positive outcomes. Given the huge positive benefits underlying the rise of offshore outsourcing, it would seem to be a no-brainer for any manager who is serious about saving costs and improving the quality of IT and IT enabled services to at least give offshoring a trial.

Good managers also have an instinctive bias for action. Since more than 200 *Fortune 500* companies have already taken the plunge and have gained positive experience, it seems obvious that the next logical step is to pick up the phone and take the plunge!

FOREWORD

BY TED FINE

Fifteen years ago, I started running a Citibank IT group which supported a number of international business units. It was my first international assignment. During the next eight years, I visited over thirty countries, working with businesses on an array of IT projects ranging from batch processing to sophisticated online systems.

Usually, my U.S.-based group and the various overseas business units operated in partnership. However, I went into these projects initially thinking we'd bear the brunt of the work and the overseas groups would tag along for the ride. After all, how could these overseas IT people be as skilled as a group of U.S. IT professionals?

One of the most significant things I learned from my international job was how wrong that preconceived judgment was; I couldn't have been more off base. What I found, in fact, were up-to-date, hard working engineers dedicated to making the businesses they worked for as successful as possible.

Of course, Citibank was a tough environment. It had all the sharp elbows, skirmishes, and turf battles we associate with any large corporation. Notwithstanding those issues, for the most part, we all worked together well, and it did not alter the respect I developed for my international colleagues. I came to realize there is a vast pool of perceptive and talented IT professionals overseas.

On many projects, the overseas teams proved to be the driving creative force, willing to take risks that my more conservative colleagues in the U.S. were unwilling to take. This reality is accounted for, at least in part, by the fact that my group worked under the close scrutiny of Citibank senior management while the overseas teams were, mercifully, thousands of miles away. These professionals were also very hard working, putting in weekends and long hours to move their projects ahead. An unusual impediment they had to deal with came from the fact that they were operating under unusual constraints imposed by their local governments. As an example, Brazil, at the time, could not import an American minicomputer.

This all made a lasting impression on me that I have never forgotten. When Atul Vohra, president of Majesco Software, asked me to join the Advisory Board of Mastek/Majesco, Inc.[1], I thought of my Citibank experience, and was very open to the idea. However, I also thought about Citibank's experiment in the 1980s with an in-house offshore IT business in India. Results were uneven and unpredictable and my fellow CIOs regarded using the Indian organization as a risky proposition, one that they were generally reluctant to try. I knew how good Indian engineers were, but wondered at that time if they had been converted into an effective, well managed organization that could be relied upon to deliver from a distance of thousands of miles.

Of course, a lot of time had passed since then, but I wondered how much progress management had made in the interim. All these thoughts were on my mind when I received Atul's invitation. I decided to visit Mastek in India before I made up my mind about joining the Board.

I had been to India before, but I was not looking at it from the perspective of a software services exporter. I saw all of the disorder we normally associate with Indian cities. I also saw an emerging middle class with the same goals and concerns of middle class Americans. Bright, young, well educated, and hard working Indian IT specialists were my guides. I remember asking a group of engineers in their mid-20s about whether their marriages were arranged. The answer was about 50/50, and

---

[1] Mastek goes by the name Majesco Software, Inc. in the U.S.

all were happily married. I will leave it to you to decide which scheme is the better. That's India today, a middle class split between the old traditions and the more modern world. This was a different India!

The Indians I met were, without exception, people I would like to have as friends and bring home to dinner (the acid test of meeting on a personal level, as far as I am concerned). They are people I would be happy to work with, an important – if not most important – dimension of any business relationship.

At Mastek, I found a highly motivated group of IT professionals. At least equally important, the software shop was very well managed and had earned a CMM-5 rating – the platinum standard for an IT organization. When I managed an IT organization in the U.S., we (along with most other U.S. IT organizations) might have been a CMM-1 shop. It's important to note that a CMM-5 rating does not happen quickly, and spending money alone will not get you there. It comes from a long-term commitment, consistent management over many years, and a drive for quality by every employee in the company. India has been on this track for at least the last decade.

In addition, the Mastek record of on-time delivery was nothing short of amazing to a former IT manager. I saw a real dedication to the people side of the business, which certainly I had not experienced very often in my career.

This description outlines my experience at Mastek, but I have no reason to believe that it was unique among Indian companies. There is no question at all that Indian IT had moved a long way from what I remembered from my days at Citibank. I returned enthused about joining Atul's board and began a three-year relationship that I have valued both personally and professionally.

Short of visiting IT vendors in India, this book is your best way to learn about Indian offshore outsourcing. It not only takes you on the trip to India, but it tells you honestly and clearly the steps you need to take to develop your offshoring program, and warns you about potential pitfalls. Atul Vohra, an experienced global manager who has worked all over the world, serves as your guide to offshoring in India and I can't think of anyone better.

Enjoy the journey!

Ted Fine

SECTION TWO

INTRODUCTION

SHALL WE DANCE?

> *"Whether you regard the trend as disruptive or benefi-
> cial, one thing is clear. Corporate America no longer
> feels it can afford to avoid India."*
> —*Business Week*, December 8, 2003*

"Now tell me exactly why we're going to India?" asked Paula Kwiker, wife of Lou Kwiker, president and CEO of ePolicy Solutions. The Kwikers were somewhere over Budapest enjoying Lufthansa's First Class service as they sped through the late afternoon to Mumbai to attend Mastek's International Customer Meeting – an opportunity to "kick the tires" and network with other clients.

"It's about learning how to synchronize work processes between my company and Mastek," Lou explained.

"What's so hard about that?" she asked.

Lou looked down at his dinner as he contemplated the complexities of a U.S.-based company working with any offshore vendor, and specifically one based in India. He wanted to explain why it was necessary to fly halfway around the world through 12-plus time zones in terms his wife could understand. She had been a professional dancer, so he asked, "Could you and another dancer synchronize a dance if a curtain was hanging between the two of you and you couldn't see each other's movements?"

"Yes, of course. Two professional dancers could do that," she said.

---

* Dallas Morning News, October 5, 2003

"Could you do it if the other dancer was from India?" Lou asked. "Could you do it if the two of you had never met before and the curtain between you was 12,000 miles thick? That's how far India is from the U.S."

His wife thought for a minute and smiled. Lou had made his point. "We probably couldn't do it unless we both had trained in the same style of dance and practiced together. Then we could dance together without being able to see one another."

ePolicy Solutions, an innovative company that sells insurance solutions, outsourced its product development to an Indian company, as have a surprising number of companies large and small – including such well-known brands as General Electric, Cisco, and Intel. Like these firms, ePolicy wanted an IT vendor that could lower costs while delivering projects faster and with higher levels of service and quality than was possible in the U.S. or anywhere else. Kwiker's company didn't just choose to outsource business functions; it wanted a "dance partner" who can help define what must be done and where best to do it to compete effectively in a tough environment.

After all, it's not just about doing things *right*, but doing the *right* things.

MAX OUT YOUR LEVERAGE

This book is about *maximizing leverage*. These may appear to be just buzzwords, but they represent a concept that brings significant depth for companies searching for sustainability and competitive advantage. A buyer of offshore services (whether in technology or business process) maximizes leverage not by squeezing the vendor's fees and rates, but by working in partnership with the vendor to create higher value for the business instead.

For example, the biggest payoff may not be in pushing for lower rates, but in doing more work offshore. Simple math proves the point. If on-site costs for work in the U.S. are $80 per hour compared to offshore costs of $20 per hour, a 10 percent improvement in offshore rates yields a savings of just $2 per hour. Yet, every additional position moved offshore produces a $60-per-hour savings.

Not just doing things right, but doing the right things. Maximizing leverage.

If maximizing leverage is the goal, then why am I, a peripatetic traveler with a business to manage, taking the time to write a book? Isn't writing a book better left for retirement?

First, the way some of my investments have been going lately makes retirement seem an awfully long time away! And, of course, I want to bring my company, Majesco, to your attention for our 15 minutes of fame. But truly a much more important reason for writing this book now, rather than in 10 or 20 years, is that India is an idea whose time has come. After centuries of languishing in the wings, India is stepping prominently onto the world economic stage. That's why I feel compelled to tell the story.

My story starts with a brief summary of the pros and cons of offshore outsourcing – or "offshoring" – and then continues in the following sections to:

- Delve more deeply into the benefits to be found offshore
- Develop an understanding of India
- Learn how to pick and manage an offshore provider
- Examine the importance of developing a partnership with your vendor and
- Explore the all-important quality movement.

Finally, I will close with some musings on what I believe the future holds. Hopefully, with this book we can begin to establish a relationship that can continue to develop through our Website and beyond. This book descends from the classical Indian tradition of the *sutradhaar*, or narrator, who forms a bridge between the audience and the drama unfolding on stage. I hope to be a bridge between U.S.-based corporations and the offshore artists.

INDIA — THE NEXT FRONTIER

I believe India represents America's next great frontier. Working together, the U.S. and India will grow exponentially stronger. As Dr. Michael Porter of the Harvard Business School wrote in *The Competitive Advantage of Nations,* "A nation's pool of human and other resources is necessarily limited. The ideal is that these resources be deployed in the most productive uses possible."[1]

India's strengths in offshoring match up well with the needs and interests and culture of the most powerful nation on Earth. As China is America's foundry, India is the back office.

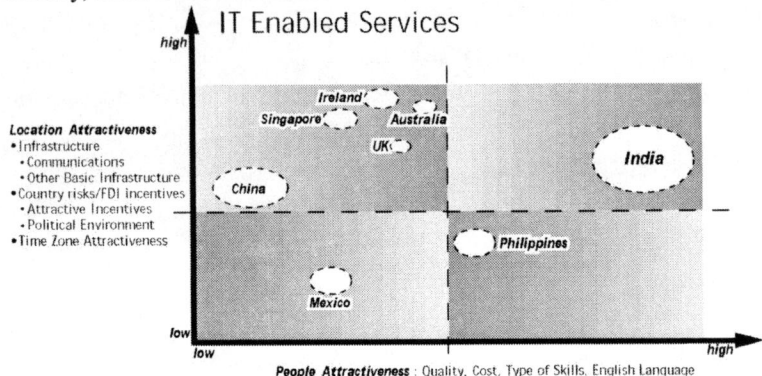

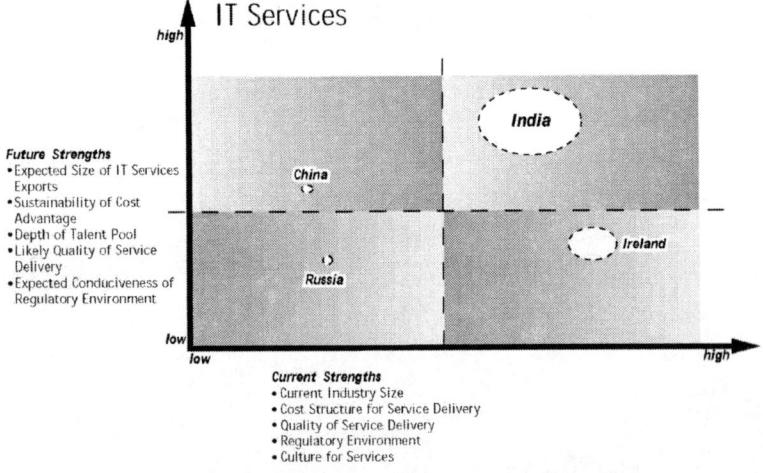

Source : McKinsey Analysis

Graphic #1: India Outstrips the Competition

India is well positioned to become the back office for America, so that America may deploy her resources most effectively elsewhere. In India, the

---

[1] Publisher: Free Press (June 1, 1998)

software industry is *the* best party in town. It attracts the best and the brightest among the graduating students in the nation. Today, an entire generation of *wunderkinder* is spread across India's software firmament. As Aroun Shourie, the country's most eminent journalist, wrote recently: "These 26/27-year-olds have changed the world's perception of India. It's not just a country of snake-charmers; it's a country against which protectionist walls have to be erected."[1]

MARCO POLO FOUND INDIA A LONG TIME AGO

For political, economic, and geographic reasons the relationship between America and India has been slow to develop. India did not seem the obvious choice. During the Cold War between capitalism and communism, India leaned more toward the Soviet geopolitical camp rather than the American camp. It took the sweeping tides of geopolitical change, the advent of the Internet with its heightened connectivity for our world, and the vision of a new generation of Indian entrepreneurs to bring these countries together.

India is an exciting country and its story, as we will see, has been in the making for millennia. From the Indus Valley civilization onwards, India's history has been tantalizingly full of twists and turns, triumphs and travails.

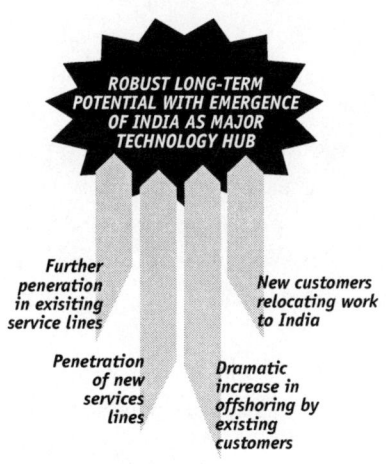

ROBUST LONG-TERM POTENTIAL WITH EMERGENCE OF INDIA AS MAJOR TECHNOLOGY HUB

Further peneration in exisiting service lines

New customers relocating work to India

Penetration of new services lines

Dramatic increase in offshoring by existing customers

Source : Nasscom-McKinsey Report 2002

Graphic #2: India's Potential

For 3,000 years invaders, explorers, traders, and peace seekers have discovered the road to India. Marco Polo found India on his way to China. Columbus was on his way to India when he discovered America.

The India story is still building. The quantitative orientation and heads-down work ethic of the Indians is thousands of years old. The English language and rule of law came with the British 300 years ago. Schools of higher learning were a result of the elitist Fabian Socialists that inherited

---

[1] Indian Express, Friday August 15, 2003

the country at its Independence 56 years back. The "brain drain" of the 1960s and '70s sowed the seeds for the India, Inc. brand and the 1990s boom when the Y2K deadline created a huge demand for Indian technologists.

Though India's competitive advantage seems meticulously planned, it follows the law of unintended consequences. The coming together of these forces may have been fortuitous; however, neither the policy makers nor the players are leaving the future to chance.

Today, American and European corporate executives are following in the footsteps of these earlier explorers and traders. Some corporate executives come looking for a deal – much like the traders of the past. Others come looking for enlightenment – a better way to run their businesses. All of them look a lot like the intellectuals of the past who came to India seeking wisdom. Each leaves significant marks on an old/young land that is destined to play a very significant role in the development of the global economy of the 21st century.

FANNING THE FLAMES

As with any new idea, there are those who feel threatened. They fear change. They lack the confidence that allows them to embrace innovation. A growing drumbeat of isolationists – who revel in reports that 1.7 million U.S. jobs, representing about $120 billion in wages, may be lost to offshore outsourcing – fuels the fear. Some forecasts appear to be even more dire. According to Forrester Research, between now and 2015, 3.3 million U.S. services industry jobs representing some $136 billion in wages will move offshore. Forrester estimates that of these jobs, 450,000 will be in the computer industry.

As bad as these predictions sound, let me put it into perspective. At even its most severe projections, the number of jobs going offshore amount to no more than one tenth of one percent of the total job market in the U.S. That is hardly even a drop in the bucket.

Yet the protectionists in America – short-term thinkers with a fear-based political agenda – step in to try to hold back the tide. The analogy of the little Dutch boy putting his finger in the dyke trying to hold back the North Sea comes to mind. A few politicians have jumped on this issue to fan the flames of their own isolationist ideology.

They are playing to fears that will not be realized. The reality is that offshoring will expand America's job market, not contract it.

A good example is Oracle, which won a contract with HP to create a database for all the medical records and many other governmental functions in a country of about a billion people. Oracle, which has been severely criticized for hiring 6,000 Indian workers, will build the database using its Indian staff. But as Larry Ellison, CEO of Oracle said recently, "They'll also be joined by the 9,000 developers at Oracle headquarters in Redwood Shores, CA, and at other Oracle work centers in Waltham, MA, and in countries other than India around the world.

"In short, the India contract is a tidy bit of new business for all of Oracle's 41,500 employees," he said.[1]

GAINS GREATER THAN THE LOSES

As it happened when the manufacturing sectors moved to less expensive markets, the U.S. economy will actually gain more than it loses from offshoring. These gains will come from reducing costs, increasing revenues, repatriating earnings, and redeploying labor.

"Offshoring brings substantial benefits to the global economy, and the lion's share will likely go to the U.S. economy," says the research by McKinsey Global Institute. "Offshoring creates wealth for U.S. companies and consumers, and therefore, for the U.S. as a whole."

For every dollar spent in moving jobs offshore, McKinsey estimates that it creates $1.12 in value within the U.S. economy. And of that $1.12 in value that returns to the U.S., 58 cents comes from savings accrued to U.S. investors and customers and 5 cents is gained when Indians import more American-made goods and services.

Providers in low-wage countries require U.S. computers, telecommunications equipment, other hardware, and software. They also buy legal, financial, and marketing services from American firms. Already, imports from the U.S. by India have grown to $3.8 billion from less than $2.5 billion as recently as 1990.

Several offshore providers serving the U.S. market are incorporated in the U.S. These companies, McKinsey argues, repatriate their earnings back to the

---

[1] Los Angeles Times, July 20, 2003

U.S. The total impact amounts to an additional 4 cents out of every dollar spent offshore.

Additional value can be generated from redeploying U.S. workers. As low value-added services are sourced from overseas vendors, U.S. workers previously engaged in providing those services are freed up to take other jobs. If redeployment continues at the rate it has over the past two decades, then for every dollar spent offshore the U.S. economy will capture an additional 45 to 47 cents from the new jobs that are generated.

THE REST OF THE STORY

What the American people are not being told – or perhaps they simply can't hear the softer voices of reason – is that the U.S. is about to face another shortage, not of jobs but of expertise. In the great tradition of radio commentator Paul Harvey, here is the rest of the story:

- Even during the recession of 2002 and 2003, the IT industry created more new jobs than it lost.
- The services sector, which includes the IT sector, of the U.S. economy loses about 10 million jobs every year, while it creates 12 million brand new ones – Michael F. Corbett & Associates, Ltd., a global sourcing consultant to Fortune 1000 companies.[1]
- By 2010, the U.S. economy will have 167 million jobs, but only 157 million people to fill them – U.S. Bureau of Labor Statistics report *"Impending Crisis: Too Many Jobs, Too Few People,"* by Roger Herman.[2]
- The world's top 100 financial institutions, most of them from the U.S., can save up to $138 billion annually in the next five to six years by moving operations to cheaper offshore locations.
- The costs of managing offshore are greater than managing next door. However, at worst these are no more than "an additional 6 percent to 10 percent," says Stephanie Overby of CIO magazine. With a payoff of more than 60 percent, the extra costs are a no-brainer.

---

[1] Putting Offshore Outsourcing in Perspective, Firmbuilders.com, July 7, 2003

[2] Publisher: Oakhill Press (October 12, 2002)

Opposition to offshore outsourcing is an understandable emotional response. But it is likely to be a short-lived phenomenon. During the 1970s and 1980s, opponents raised similar complaints against the movement of most computer and semiconductor manufacturing operations out of the U.S. to other locations such as Taiwan and Southeast Asia.

These moves had little long-term impact on the U.S. technology community as engineering, marketing, and other management positions replaced factory positions. Some economists credit the massive economic expansion of the late 1990s to the freeing up of some of America's finest minds to innovate, design, and ultimately manage new ventures.

OPENING NEW MARKETS

A common mistake is forgetting that globalization is a two-way street. It is a driving force in the strength of the U.S. economy. American companies currently make up about 70 percent of all IT exports from India. In turn, Indian IT companies employ more than 60,000 people in the United States. These employees of Indian companies buy goods and services each year that total more than $1 billion in value.

In India the middle class – defined as anyone who earns at least $1,800 annually – is growing very rapidly. In 2003, the middle class is growing at a rate of 17 percent and projected to hit almost 25 percent in less than five years. As a result, *Time* magazine reports that many household name brand companies from America and Europe are beating down the doors to get to India. The economic growth allows for increased American exports to India, where young people and their parents can be seen shopping the malls for some of the world's strongest brands.

Globalization also keeps costs down, helping American companies stay competitive and freeing up financial resources for more strategic investment. The National Association of Software and Services Companies (NASSCOM), the leading software trade association in India, estimates that the U.S. economy is saving $10 to $11 billion by outsourcing work to India in 2003 alone.

NASSCOM

WHAT IS NASSCOM?

National Association of Software and Service Companies (NASSCOM) is the apex chamber of commerce for IT software and service organizations in India. The chamber is the voice of the Indian IT industry, nationally and internationally and its membership, which exceeds 800, represents players from all segments viz. IT software & services, e-commerce, internet, R&D and ITES & BPO spanning private and public sectors and include homegrown as well as multi-nationals.

NASSCOM represents the Indian IT fraternity at WITSA (World Information Technology Services Alliance) and ASOCIO (Asian Oceanian Computing Industry Organisation). Further, the association partners with the world's best research and consultancy organizations like McKinsey, Harvard etc to provide a two-way flow of information - within the country to its members on Global trends and internationally to the key markets about Indian IT industry.

As the representative body of the IT industry, NASSCOM works closely with the Indian Central & State governments to formulate policies and strategies for the advancement of this sector locally as well as internationally. Also importantly, one of its key functions is to build global brand equity for the Indian software and service Industry.

NASSCOM CHARTER

* Maintaining close interaction with the Government of India in formulating National IT policies with specific focus on IT software and services
* Maintaining a state of the art information database of IT software and services related activities for use of both the software developers as well as interested companies overseas.
* Encourage members to provide world-class quality products, services and solutions in India and overseas and help build brand equity for the Indian IT software and services industry.
* Taking effective steps to campaign against software piracy.
* Provide an ideal forum for overseas and domestic companies to explore the vast potential available for Joint Ventures, Strategic Alliances, Marketing Alliances, Joint Product Development, etc., by organising Business Meets with delegations of various countries.
* Work actively with Overseas Governments, Embassies to make the Visa and Work Permit Rules more "India Industry Friendly".
* Disseminate various policies, market information and other relevant statistics by sending more than 200 circulars (annually) to all members.
* Involve membership participation in various forums of Nasscom on subjects such as HRD, Technology, Exports, Domestic Market, E-Governance, IT Enabled Services, IPR, Finance, Government Policies, Quality, etc.

Graphic #3: Nasscom represents Indian software solutions and services companies and sets policies for the industry

DEFINE THE CORE COMPETENCIES

Once a company decides to move forward with outsourcing, the two big challenges are figuring out what to outsource and how to manage the resulting organizational structure. Regarding what to outsource, the important work is clearly defining the company's core competitive advantage. For businesses that are highly dependent on technology, other important considerations are the rate of change of technology and the need for customer intimacy. Essentially, most information technology and business processes are mission critical, but are not necessarily the defining core competency of an enterprise.

Companies are in for a rude shock if they think that their responsibility is over when they hire an outsource vendor. Offshoring isn't about handing your problems off to someone else to manage. The challenge is to establish a solid connection with your chosen vendor and to build a governance structure that can elevate the bond between the two companies from a client/vendor relationship to a true partnership. I dedicate an entire section of this book to this all-important commitment that ensures alignment of goals and can carry the companies successfully through the twists and turns that are inevitable parts of any relationship.

Above all else, expansion in offshoring will build the global economy and serve the long-term needs of the American economy – and America's companies – well.

Ultimately, that's the reason I decided to write this book – with the strong support of my company and its founders – because we want to share the recipe of how to succeed in coming to India.

Through the medium of this book, we can spread our experience and knowledge to many more people than I can physically call on and speak to. We are a transparent company and truly believe that our role is to help American and European executives understand India – its strengths and its weaknesses – and to take you, the reader, from *knowing* to *doing*. I'll share some additional thoughts on this topic in the final section of this book.

On a personal note, I am passionate about this book because I am passionate about globalization. I am a product of globalization and have seen the incredible benefits that come from mixing cultures and experiences. I have spent about a third of my 24-year career in assignments on each of three continents, zigzagging back and forth among three distinct cultures.

The first eight years after college were in India, my birthplace. The last 16 years I have worked alternately in Europe (mostly in Greece and Hungary) or in the U.S.

I speak both Hindi and English, but never felt any constraints in Greece or Hungary due to language issues. In fact, I have found language is seldom a significant constraint. The reason is simple. The yearnings of the mind, and feelings of the heart and the gut, are universal.

In my previous assignments, these universal yearnings enabled us to produce Bass footwear . . . to grow mushrooms for Ragu sauces . . . and build Citibank's banking business in India based on deposits from overseas Indians funding loans in their home country. Many of these cross-border flows helped build an awareness and skill set on both the 'buy' and the 'sell' side. Those experiences, combined with the interconnected nature of today's society, make it possible to think big – very big.

Thanks to these experiences, I find it easy to dream that India can be a true partner of America and the American corporation – that India can be the back office of the world. I absolutely believe that Information Technology and Information Technology Enabled Services will catapult India into a modern, economically sound global leader.

Who Should Read This Book?

I wrote this book to address those corporate executives who have a desire and a need to understand India, and who want to know how to use India's assets to create a sustainable competitive advantage for their companies.

I believe senior executives from small, medium, and large corporations alike who read this book will gain new insights into the possibilities of offshore outsourcing, or "offshoring." I hope there is at least one "ah, ha" that jumps off the page at you. I am confident that many readers will have their eyes opened to the incredible possibilities that India offers.

In addition, I believe this book can serve as a reference guide on how to offshore IT and IT-enabled services projects. Readers will learn the essential steps involved in building a strategic relationship with an Indian partner.

And for still other readers this book may be a wake-up call on how to best use global resources while building on core competencies in the U.S. This book is a call to action for U.S. companies – and indeed for the U.S. economy at large – as they develop new business approaches that require a new mind-set and resources unlike any they have used heretofore.

Each company has its own need for speed, quality, and sustainability. The most likely readers will be corporate chief information officers (CIOs), and at times I talk directly to CIOs. I hope this book brings new insight into how CIOs can manage some of these challenges. Also, I hope it will educate other senior executives – from board chairmen to the chief executive officers, from chief financial officers to line senior managers – about the challenges involved in putting IT to work solving real business problems. While all levels of management will hopefully gain from this book, it is especially written for those who are globally curious. It is my desire that every reader takes away from this book a new understanding about India and its ability to be the partner for which their corporation is looking.

Outsourcing overseas is not without its risks. There are risks in selecting an offshore vendor that can deliver a high quality project on budget and on time. There are political risks that seem to shift constantly. There is the need to protect the privacy of corporate data and intellectual property. There are risks – perceived and real – of control, cyber terrorism, and cultural incompatibility. This book will explore each of these risks, as well as the opportunities available to corporations that choose to outsource their IT and IT-enabled services work to India.

WHAT THIS BOOK TRIES TO DO

The contents of this book may surprise you. It covers the advantages of offshoring to India in depth. In the first section, the book explores the advantages of offshoring to India, including lower costs, higher quality, and the predictable quality and timeliness of the work. In the second section, the book draws upon many of my personal experiences to provide an insider's guide to India itself – its strengths, weaknesses, and contradictions.

Then the book turns to the nuts and bolts of the offshoring process. The third section provides a guide to selecting an outsourcing vendor – ideally a true partner – and to managing that relationship. I hope I can persuade you that it is far better to build a partnership with an Indian firm than simply to hire a vendor.

Next, the book analyzes the critical issue of quality. In the future, when we look back at this era in business, I expect that the compelling reason for outsourcing work to India will *not* be cost savings, as much as the *higher quality* work produced by the CMM-5 qualified firms that dot the landscape in India.

Finally, the book looks toward the future. I hope this section will stimulate some thoughts of your own about where our world is going, the global nature of the world economy, and some opportunities you may seize for your own career.

There is much I do not cover. Some aspects, such as legal issues and contracting, frankly are best left to others who are more competent in these areas. Also, I do not try to analyze the strengths and weaknesses of other countries, like Ireland and China. These countries and others also present tremendous opportunities for American business. But I was always told to write about what I know. And what I know is India and how American companies can best work with their Indian counterparts.

I do not claim to offer any great new methodology. There are no new acronyms. Rather, there is a lot of practical advice and a few stories that should be of great interest. In addition, I ask that you read this book with pen in hand. It should create the opportunity for you to ask some very pointed questions of your own IT staff.

ABOUT MASTEK

My company, Mastek, is a software solutions and services company. Headquartered in India, Mastek has development centers in Mumbai and Pune equipped with the hardware and software necessary for complex software development projects. It also operates independent subsidiaries in the U.S., where it is known as Majesco Software (regrettably the word

Mastek was already taken). The company also operates in Great Britain, Germany, Singapore, and Japan. Mastek stock trades on the major stock exchanges in India.

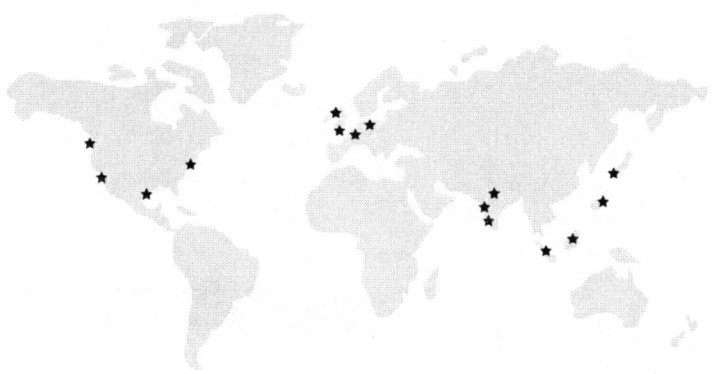

Graphic #4: Mastek Worldwide: Like many Indian firms, Mastek is located in multiple countries in Asia, Europe and North America

Mastek was founded in 1982 by four business school friends who wanted to build a company that merged management, strategy, and technology (hence the name Mastek). With an initial investment of $160, the four young men – Ashank, Ketan, Sundar, and Sudhakar – launched Mastek with a passion to build a superior IT company. The founders still lead the company today and will for the foreseeable future. In fact, most Indian IT companies are still run by their founders. This is such a young industry; the generational transfer of power has not yet occurred.

I once heard a savvy American businessman remark that, if the margins in the technology business continued to be as slim as they are, he would do better owning a chain of coffee and donut shops. Of course, there are days we all would like to chuck in the towel. And the opportunity costs of staying in the technology business may be very high, when compared to other industries. But when you visit India, what you will hear from the founders of most Indian companies is that they cannot imagine doing anything else.

The men who founded these companies and built an industry have only one passion: to build software. They have ridden the ups and downs of the stock markets without changing their core businesses. The financial numbers were purely an outcome of what they set themselves out to do, which was to build software and a great place to work. At the risk of sounding over-sentimental, an air of mysticism pervades most Indian companies. It is not just the leaders, but the rank and file as well who talk of their "larger purpose."

Today Mastek ranks 13th among Indian IT firms. It was selected by *Forbes* magazine as one of the top 200 small businesses (revenues under $1 billion) in the world.

When you visit us in India – and you have a standing invitation – I think you will be amazed at the attitude and professionalism you will find among our employees. To a person, the Mastekeers (as they call themselves) believe they are destined for far greater things because they are delivering real value to their customers. Their enthusiasm can be deafening at times, yet is typical of the bullishness attitude you will find among Indian IT companies.

We hope you will share in our bullish approach to business, and life!

SECTION THREE

Why Offshore

"If the Cold War had been a sport, it would have been sumo wrestling. If globalization were a sport, it would be a 100-meter dash, over and over and over."
— Tom Friedman, New York Times columnist and author*

In today's corporate world the Chief Information Officer (CIO) has come a long way in a very short time. As recently as the early 1990s, the CIO position existed in only a few corporations. There were MIS, IT, and ERP managers or directors, but few executives with the authority and responsibilities now placed on the shoulders of the corporate CIO. In the past, the IT director usually reported to the CFO or the Head of Operations.

Today, the CIO often reports directly to the CEO, and some are even moving up to assume the CEO position. Tony Comper, the CEO of Bank of Montreal, is an example of a CIO who made the move. Michael Capellas – currently CEO of MCI – first joined Compaq Computer as CIO before becoming CEO and engineering Compaq's merger with Hewlett-Packard. There are more such highly qualified executives in line to move into the

*The Lexus and The Olive Tree, Publisher- Farrar, Strauss & Giroux (June 2000)

top management position as CIOs gain recognition for their strategic contributors to the corporate management team.

And the enlarging role of the CIO is not just limited to the large corporations. A recent article in *The American Banker* pointed out that CIOs are becoming far more influential in mid-sized companies as well.

As with any senior executive position, the CIO faces tremendous and complex pressures. The CIO must deliver high quality products that work as promised the first time, keep current with the latest releases, and provide innovation and flexibility to businesses processes . . . and do it all within an increasingly constrained cost structure. In addition, the CIO must build happy, motivated teams and visibly contribute to corporate success.

All these pressures – whether external or generated by CIOs them-selves – have prompted some wags to say that the initials CIO really stand for "Career is Over."

THE TOUGHEST JOB IN BUSINESS

The CIO position is one of the most analyzed, surveyed, and dissected job titles in America. It is rare to pick up a copy of *ComputerWorld*, *InfoWorld,* or *Network World* and not find an analysis of the plight of the CIO. A recent issue of *InfoWorld* blazoned a headline: "Do you feel safe yet?"[1] Only the Chief Executive Officer position is dissected as often.

Chad Dickerson, Chief Technology Officer for *InfoWorld* magazine, wrote recently in the magazine that CIOs are much like the sound manag-ers for a rock band. "Run (the sound) well, and hardly anyone notices. Do it poorly, and the wrath of the audience and band is upon you."

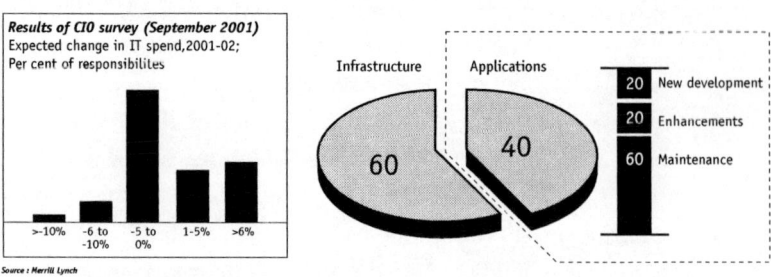

Graphic #5: Technology Spending

---

[1] Pros and Cons of Invisible IT: Chad Dickerson, Infoworld.com, July 25, 2003

The IT infrastructure and the people who run it are integral to the success of every enterprise. The CIO is the center of the vortex. Without a strong IT department, most businesses will fail or fall far behind. But too often, people take the CIO position for granted – much like the soundman of a rock band.

The CIO must also focus more on driving the corporation's strategic business needs and is far more integrated into the senior management team where business decisions take precedence over technology speeds and feeds. Marianne Broadbent, a Gartner vice president, told *CIO Insight*: "The job is different now in some places, less tech-oriented and more strategy focused. The purely technical CIO, as we have known it, is disappearing."

The CIO today needs, as a friend's ski coach told me, "both soft eyes and hard eyes." The soft eyes scan the terrain ahead, looking for moguls and other obstacles. The hard eyes help negotiate the immediate bends and turns.

From my work day in and day out with CIOs and their teams, it is clear that the challenges most CIOs face are daunting. They must:

- Ensure systems availability
- Deliver projects on time
- Stay current with new developments in technology
- Manage costs aggressively to minimize budgets
- Recruit, motivate, and manage creative people
- Drive innovation and strategic thinking
- Align IT to empower business success

CIO's Top Priorities

42% of healthcare CIOs chose "aligning IT" as a priority, significantly above norm	Total	under 1,000 employees	under 1,000 employees
Aligning IT with the business needs	31.7%	28.9%	36.4%
Making the enterprise more adaptive, flexible and faster	18.4	18.6	18.2
Developing strategies that leverage new technologies	13.6	14.9	11.9
Ensuring security and business continuity	11.9	14.0	8.4
Ensuring projects are completed on time and on budget	10.1	9.5	11.2
Reducing costs	6.0	3.7	9.8
Helping to launch new products or lines of business	5.2	6.6	2.8
Ensuring systems uptime	1.8	2.5	0.7
Recruiting, retaining, developing staff	0.3	0.4	0.0

Source : CIO Insight 2003

Graphic #6: CIO – The Toughest Job

In addition to all these challenges, the CIO must keep those crazy, demanding guys in the business units happy. At the end of the day, what matters most is that the business unit executives believe that the IT department is delivering the tools and data they need. The problem, of course, is that the average business manager doesn't understand the real demands on the CIO, (i.e. that everyone says everything needed to be done yesterday.) This means the CIO needs to become an expert in the company's business and strategies in order to communicate with business unit managers and help them understand IT within the business context.

So, How Do You Win? By Looking East..

The key question becomes how do we reduce the pressures weighing on CIOs and help them help their companies in a highly competitive, rapidly changing world economy? If you look to the same old vendors, you will get the same old answers. To stay in the game – much less gain a competitive edge – you must think differently. By all means, keep control of the process, but look to the East for answers. Look to India, where a vast pool of very talented young IT professionals stand poised to do your heavy lifting.

In India you will find new friends eager to help – a strategic partner (or partners) that can help solve many, if not all, of your most complex IT challenges. Your new partners in India will deliver your projects at lower cost, with a higher level of quality and on a predictable schedule.

For many, India may seem a long way to go to make new friends, especially when there are so many 'alternative' shores talked about every day. There are potential new friends closer – in Canada, Mexico, Ireland, or even the Caribbean. I am probably less biased than you might suspect, and I am confident I can make the case that India is the answer.

The Offshore Trend

The move toward offshore outsourcing has strong momentum in all business sectors today. In 1990, few, if any, U.S. corporations outsourced their IT work offshore. Today, more than 300 of the Fortune 500 firms do business with Indian IT services companies, according to Gartner. The research firm predicts that by 2004, more than 80 percent of U.S companies will have considered using offshore IT services.

Research firms are stepping over one another to predict incredible growth for outsourcing offshore. Here is just a sampling:

- Aberdeen Group estimates that Indian companies control 85 to 90 percent of the total offshore development market.
- Forrester Research found that 44 percent of all large U.S. firms (with revenues of $1 billion or greater) now outsource IT work overseas, either to a foreign vendor or to a captive unit on foreign soil. That percentage, Forrester says, will grow to 67 percent in the next few years.
- McKinsey & Associates said, "India has consolidated its position as the pre-eminent destination for IT services and IT-enabled services. Based on current strengths and long-term potential, India scores over Ireland, Russia, China, and other competing services destinations." McKinsey forecasts that the Indian software industry will hit $57 billion in export revenues by 2008 and have between $70 and $80 billion in total revenues.
- Gartner Group agrees: "India is still the leader in the off-shore programming industry and the country that a large number of enterprises go to when outsourcing application development and maintenance."

	Custom Application Development	Application Outsourcing
Total Market Size US$ bn	18	11
India's Market Share 2000; %	13.6	15.8
Market Size 2008 US$ bn	20-25	20-25
Export Aspiration 2008 US $ bn	7.8-8.0	7.0-7.2
Global Market Share Assumption 2008; %	30-35	30-35

Source : Nasscom-McKinsey Report 2002

Graphic #7: India's Share of the Application Services Market Worldwide

India is approaching a dominant position in the outsourced offshore market. Its strengths – the size of its professional labor force, widespread fluency in English, the proven quality of deliverables, accommodation and stability of government/political conditions, and protection of intellectual property – make India increasingly the safe – and the right – choice.

THE GLOBAL TECHNOLOGY HUB

Hubs – points of concentration – have emerged across many industries. In manufacturing the hubs are in Mexico, Taiwan, and China. In the entertainment industry, Hollywood and New York reign. And the hubs for information technology are in the U.S., Japan, and India.

Recently, I heard a comedian comment that we drink French wine and buy Japanese electronics . . . but we don't drink Japanese wine or buy French electronics. That's one value of a hub; it is self-perpetuating.

Concentration of talent, successful branding, infusion of capital, and knowledge sharing can drive a virtuous cycle of growth. When these factors are concentrated in one place – as they are in India for software development – that location becomes a hub.

History clearly demonstrated this phenomenon. China has emerged as the consumer goods manufacturing hub. It has a 30 percent share in air conditioners, 24 percent share in washing machines, and a 16 percent

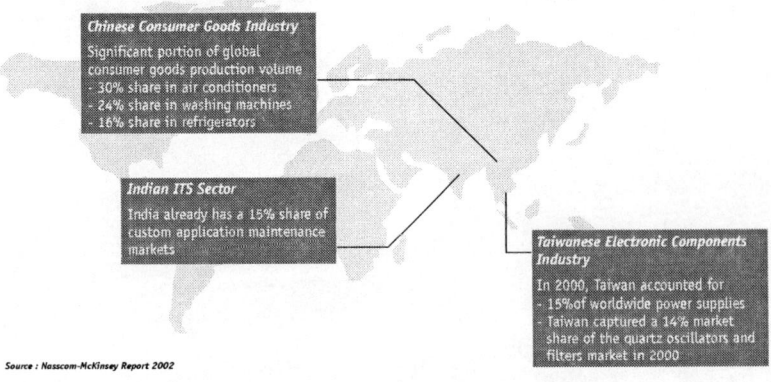

Source : Nasscom-McKinsey Report 2002

Graphic #8: Global Technology Hubs – China has captured a dominant share of consumer goods manufacturing, Taiwan in electronics; India in software services

share in refrigerators. Taiwan has a similar story in the electronics compo-nents industry. In 2000, Taiwan accounted for around 15 percent of world-wide power supplies as well as a 14 percent share of the quartz oscillators and filters market.

In comparison, India has captured a 15 percent market share in the worldwide application service business. Clearly, India has the potential to emerge as a hub for all IT services. Like Chinese manufacturing, the Indian back office position is strong and growing stronger.

No business trend can sustain a growth curve like offshore outsourcing is experiencing without providing a solid foundation of service that solves many of the challenges CIOs face today. Of course, we have all witnessed the "herd mentality" in business – those times when business after busi-ness jump on a trend and ride it to success or disaster. This trend is build-ing strong momentum and is likely to continue well into the future.

One reason offshore outsourcing is gaining such momentum is sim-ply that it solves many of the problems CIOs face today.

How Can India Make You a Hero?

When You Go East, Costs Go South

The Challenge: Cut costs across the board; build best-in-class flexibility.

The Solution: Build a strategic partnership with an Indian firm to cut overall costs and allow flexibility and benchmarking.

In every survey of CIOs today, the pressure to contain costs tops the list of their most pressing concerns. Business boom and bust cycles make normal cost containment pressures worse. The promise is to cut costs now and spend later. But even when business returns to higher levels of growth, it's unlikely that CIOs will have flush budgets. IT cost containment is a fact of business life; CIOs must perform at higher levels with smaller budgets.

It is a mantra I hear from my friends who sit in board rooms of large corporations again and again: Corporate leaders will never allow IT bud-gets to grow unchecked. All IT projects will be subject to a clear benchmarking process to demonstrate that the end results will be worth the investment.

A Cheaper Source of Code

Normalized cost structure, percent of costs

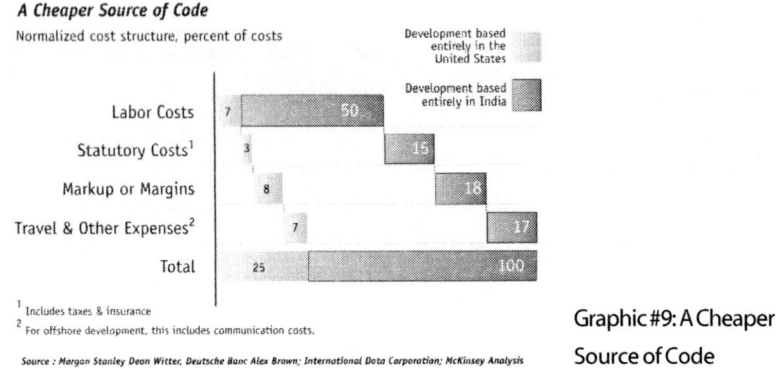

Labor Costs

Statutory Costs[1]

Markup or Margins

Travel & Other Expenses[2]

Total

[1] Includes taxes & insurance
[2] For offshore development, this includes communication costs.

Source : Morgan Stanley Dean Witter, Deutsche Banc Alex Brown; International Data Corporation; McKinsey Analysis

Graphic #9: A Cheaper Source of Code

IT'S NOT CHEAP . . . JUST LESS EXPENSIVE

Outsourcing to an Indian firm cuts costs immediately and will continue to contain costs substantially for years to come due to the lower wage rates in India and the number of young professionals graduating each year from India's top universities and institutes. The savings from working with an Indian firm result from lower base labor costs, lower benefits costs, higher average number of hours worked each week, and greater productivity in general.

As the graphic above illustrates, base salary is obviously the largest differentiator. This alone routinely translates into 80 to 85 percent in savings. There is also a substantial saving in taxes and insurance costs, as well as lower general administration and margins.

There are, of course, some areas where you will incur additional costs in taking work offshore. The primary added cost is for travel and, to a lesser extent, communications. These two budget items usually increase costs about 10 percent for travel and 2 percent for communications, when compared to continuing to do the work in-house in the U.S.

But given the magnitude of the salary and general expense differentials, these extra costs hardly make a dent in the overall savings.

The bottom line is that offshoring to India represents potential sav-

> The costs of communications have been coming down steadily. Prices for capacity between major cities in the U.S. and Europe have fallen about 70 percent annually in each of the last three years. For example, two years ago an OC-3 (155 Mbps) circuit between New York and Los Angeles cost $1.8 million per year. By the first quarter of 2002, the same lease could be had for less than $150,000.
>
> Transoceanic fiber capacity grew from near zero in 1990 to about 30 Gbps across the Atlantic and about 25 Gbps across the Pacific by 1996. By 2001, that capacity had grown to about 1,850 Gbps across the Atlantic and 345 Gbps across the Pacific. Plans are in place to reach 4,775 Gbps capacity across the Atlantic and almost 2,400 Gbps capacity across the Pacific by 2004. This rapid growth in capacity is driving the cost of telecommunications down.

ings from 40 to 60 percent since there needs to be a mix of onsite and offshore activity. Hourly rates in India range from $20 to $30 an hour compared to the U.S., where they vary from $70 to $100 per hour. Also, there is no overtime paid for more than 40 hours a week in India. Even with the added cost of remote project management, these labor rates give tremendous savings.

These rates are sustainable for the foreseeable future and will continue throughout much of the 21st century simply because the Indian labor pool is virtually bottomless. The number of graduates from high quality universities and technical institutes totals about 200,000 per year. Surprised? Don't be. IT is

Category	2000-01	2001-02	2002-03	2003-04	2004-05
IT Professionals from degree & diploma colleges	74,364	90,867	99,959	110,495	115,533
Non-IT Professionals from degree & diploma colleges	32,025	35,612	38,423	43,261	55,877
IT labor from non-engineering fields	26,597	31,620	34,595	38,439	42,853
New IT labor	132,986	158,099	172,977	192,194	214,263
Total number of Engineering seats	290,088	333,094	361,076	401,791	464,743

Source : Nasscom

Graphic # 10: Number of Indian IT Professionals

the best party in town, so why wouldn't many bright, young Indians want to join the party?

Working with an Indian firm also allows the harried CIO to exchange fixed costs of staff, equipment, and space leases for totally variable costs. Cutting costs out of a fixed-cost base is not enough. The fixed cost base makes it hard to adjust spending to match the ups and downs of business cycles. The demand to lower costs makes it tough for CIOs to meet the other demands of the business.

Now the CIO can do zero-based budgeting. When you outsource, you pay only for what you need, when you need it. Every year the CIO can take a project to zero and require the vendor to justify costs. That is very difficult to do in the U.S.

Offshoring allows you to adjust staff levels to match business needs and cost demands without the complex, difficult, and time-consuming process of hiring or firing in-house staff. The flexibility to move to a variable cost environment is invaluable. In fact, the added flexibility realized with offshore outsourcing perhaps is of as much value as the outright cost reductions.

In addition to being less expensive and more flexible, working with an Indian partner can help resolve some nagging issues of measurement and benchmarking. Indian firms have developed extensive, highly effective benchmarking skills to quantify their claims that they provide higher quality work at an affordable price.

The CIO must develop flexible business models that can deliver higher quality work in record time without having to hire additional staff. During the go-go years of the 1990s, IT departments and software providers in the U.S. lost credibility as companies grossly overspent. Many were caught up in marketing hype fueled by the "dot com" craze. A recent study by Gartner Inc. and Morgan Stanley concluded that 20 percent of the $2.7 trillion spent worldwide annually on IT is wasted.

Even worse, much of the money spent produced little in the way of tangible results. Millions of lines of code lie unused. In some cases, licenses for products are like the stock of their issuing companies – virtually worthless.

Why such a poor track record? If you ask most senior executives, the answer is that the losses were due to project delays and needless software and hardware purchases. A lot of companies rushed to get the latest hot new technology, only to spend too much, fail to implement it properly, or underestimate how long it would take to get it all up and running.

In the future – even in the face of a coming IT development boom – such a poor track record will not be tolerated again. Efficiency, performance tuning, benchmarking, adjustable budgets, lower costs, and a demand for the highest possible quality will be the driving forces.

THE BEST NEVER REST

The Challenge: Deliver the highest quality work.

The Solution: Work with a CMM Level 5 firm that has proven its
                ability to deliver the highest quality work.

Number of SEI-CMM Level 5 Companies

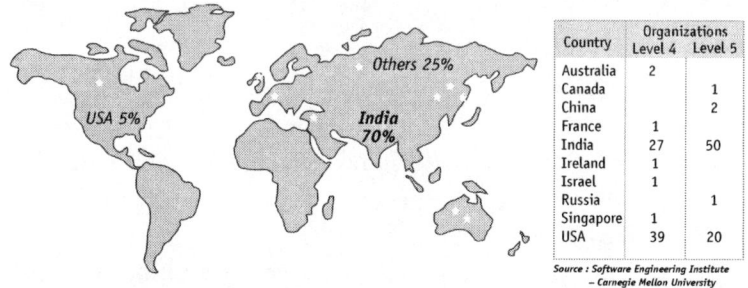

Country	Organizations Level 4	Organizations Level 5
Australia	2	
Canada		1
China		2
France	1	
India	27	50
Ireland	1	
Israel	1	
Russia		1
Singapore	1	
USA	39	20

Source : Software Engineering Institute
– Carnegie Mellon University

Graphic #11: Number of SEI-CMM Level 5 Companies—Indian firms have taken a leadership position in achieving SEI-CMM Level 5 status

The quality of IT work being produced in India equals or surpasses that of the U.S. The large number of Indian firms that have adopted the strenuous disciplines inherent in the Capability Maturity Model (CMM) has turned the phrase "Made in India" into a badge of honor for millions of young Indian business professionals. Of the 74 companies worldwide that have attained Level 5 of the CMM process, 50 are in India. Working with an experienced software shop will improve your operation.

High quality software pays big dividends, the most obvious of which is lowering the level of rework required. It also greatly reduces the effort needed to maintain the software over its life, a significant cost saving.

Perhaps most importantly, it plays a pivotal role in producing a high performance and high availability system operation. Companies simply cannot achieve true 24x7 operations without the highest quality software. A less obvious, yet important, side benefit comes when in-house staff learn the management and measurement techniques used to produce high quality software.

A full discussion of quality and its impact on profitability is found in Section 6. Achieving CMM-level 5 is a very steep climb, but it is not likely to be the IT world's Mount Everest. CMM and quality are not destinations; quality is a never-ending journey.

THE FAST AND THE FURIOUS

The Challenge: Deliver completed projects on time.
The Solution: Use an offshore company that delivers predictably and quickly.

In the movie *Top Gun*, actor Tom Cruise's fighter pilot character says in an oft-quoted line: "I feel the need for speed!" Most CIOs can relate to this. They want the IT equivalent of putting their programmers in the cockpit of a fighter jet catapulting them off an aircraft carrier, accelerating to Mach 1 in seconds.

Lower costs and higher quality are meaningless if the work is not produced on schedule. Speed is the critical third factor. Too often, corporate IT departments are their own worst enemy; they miss too many deadlines. In most businesses, any new product or service launch depends on IT to support supply chain logistics and other product requirements. But time is finite. Projects have deadlines – sometimes impossible deadlines. On-time delivery by the IT group is a critical success factor.

Reliability is a function of processes that enable predictable on-time delivery. Speed is also made possible by depth of resources. Indian firms typically offer a depth of resources and ability to scale rapidly. With lower costs, the Indian IT industry is able (and has the good sense) to carry a deep bench and invest in extensive professional training. Typically service firms in India operate at 70 to 80 percent utilization versus 90 percent plus in the U.S. Our company, for example, invests in five weeks of training per person, per year. Five days are more often the case in the U.S.

Being 12 time zones away has some disadvantages, but Indian companies have turned the tyranny of distance into an asset. The time zone differential makes round-the-clock development and service possible without the problems common to second and third shifts. Speed comes from following the sun. While Americans are sleeping, Indians are writing and testing code. Most CIOs we work with come to work in the morning excited at the prospect of seeing what their Indian partner produced overnight.

Some business gurus will tell you that in today's fast moving world, the key strategic factor for any business is the ability to respond to customer needs quickly and efficiently. There is constant pressure on today's CIO to speed up deliveries.

In writing about globalization, *New York Times* columnist and Pulitzer Prize-winning author Tom Friedman says globalization has replaced the Cold War as the new defining system. This system is about speed and time-to-market rather than the size of arsenals. It's about fast fish eating slower fish, not necessarily bigger eating smaller.

The telecommunications industry saw the need for speed and depth early in the game. The telecommunications giants found themselves in a highly competitive environment following deregulation of the phone industry. Long distance companies wanted to jump into the local calling market, previously the exclusive domain of the Baby Bells. In turn, the local provider companies wanted to compete for lucrative long distance markets.

To compete in this race, one telecommunications company approached us to help build a customer front end capability. The client company chose Seibel's Scopus system due to its functionality, but extensive customization was required. Not only were the challenges of customizing Scopus to meet the requirements complex, but also the entire project needed to be completed in record time.

Mastek/Majesco, working with Deloitte Consulting, drew on resources in our development center in India. We were intimately familiar with Scopus since we staffed the Scopus help desk for Seibel. We ramped up the project very quickly, deploying 150 full-time equivalent programmers within 45 days. As a result, the telecommunications client was able to launch its services in record time.

KEEP YOUR PUNCHED-CARD READER UP-TO-DATE

The Challenge: Maintain all application and system software with the latest revision levels.

The Solution: Use an Indian supplier to plan and integrate a release update schedule using their knowledge of your software suppliers' plans.

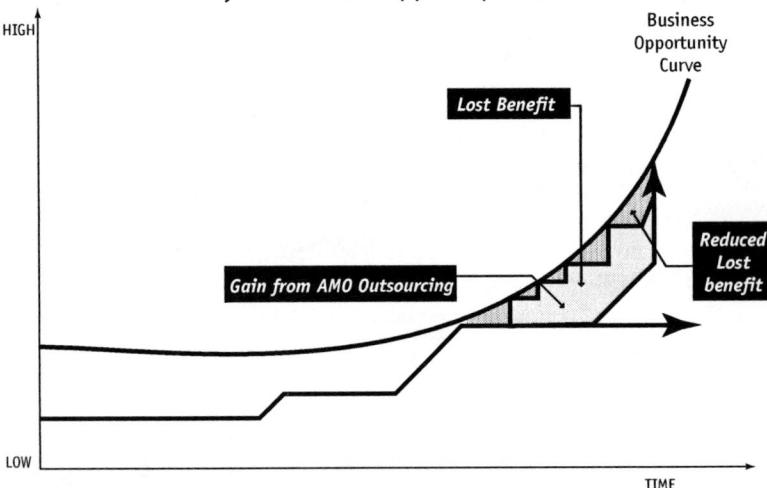

Graphic #12: Benefits of Application Maintenance Outsourcing – Timely and continuous maintenance enhance an application's life, efficiency and scope

Most corporate IT systems are a complex set of homegrown applications, licensed software packages, multiple operating systems, and an amalgam of middleware software. All these systems must be maintained and kept up to date. Failure to stay current with a software vendor's latest release levels can soon render your system unable to accept upgrades and enhancements. This part of the CIOs job is rather like servicing a Boeing 747 jetliner . . . while it's in flight. You have to keep your pilot's and mechanic's licenses up to date!

For most businesses, just keeping current with the steady stream of updated releases from vendors like Cisco or IBM is expensive to maintain. But failure to stay current is even more expensive. It is like the old saying: "You can pay me now . . . or pay me more later."

Look at a quick snapshot of the issue. Between 1998 and 2002, one top CRM product vendor launched four new major versions. Three of these versions entailed either a major architectural change or data model re-design. Within each version four sub-releases came out before the subsequent version. In between all this, two more versions were layered across sub-releases. In addition, there were anywhere from 10 to 75 patches, and the time between two major releases was never more than 18 months.

Similarly, another major vendor – after making an acquisition in January 2001 – released five major versions (15 releases for Tools and five for CRM product) in just over two years.

Release schedules like these are not uncommon. Typically, a corporate IT organization must deal with some sort of change or upgrade on a monthly basis. Maintaining in-house resources dedicated to keeping up-to-speed with these ever-changing releases and patches is a difficult challenge. Many companies often skip or delay upgrades due to the cost and practical difficulties of keeping up with the changes.

We watched the impact of this basic issue unfold in the summer of 2003. The lesson of the Blackout of 2003 in the northeastern U.S. is that maintenance may not be sexy, and it can be very expensive. But the cost of maintenance pales in comparison to shutting down the entire electrical grid across multiple states and Canadian provinces. Maintenance of the electrical grid was too long neglected. As a result, a relatively minor glitch in one part of the system plunged the entire Northeastern Grid into overload.

Since Indian outsourcing firms work with multiple clients running a staggering array of disparate systems, it's imperative for them to keep abreast of the latest technology and maintain their systems. As a result, most Indian companies make substantial investments in research and development (R&D). Equipment failure is not an option for an Indian firm. That fact is one reason that many Indian firms, including my own, replace and upgrade equipment every two years. That is much faster than corporations which don't think of the IT department as a front office – as Indian vendors do.

Another example: the media are paying increasing attention to the advent of the 64-bit processors that will power next generation PCs. These greatly enhanced processors will increase capabilities exponentially. IBM claims its new processors can support more than 200 in-flight instructions at a time – a 71 percent increase – and 4 billion times more memory than the 32-bit Pentium 4. Despite this, many U.S. firms will move slowly to purchase expensive new systems based on these processors.

Not so in India. Indian IT firms will be among the first to acquire the latest technology and will quickly build expertise in implementing this exciting next generation technology . . . expertise that will be very useful for their American clients.

Why will Indian companies move to 64-bit architectures faster than their U.S. counterparts? For several reasons. First, Indian firms depreciate their equipment over a much shorter time frame than U.S. firms. They also have a greater incentive to use the most effective technology in their software development to reduce time and cost – their stock and trade. And finally, the R&D departments for Indian firms are charged with staying up-to-date on new developments in technology. If they do not, the firms are not as valuable to their client partners and risk falling behind their aggressive competitors.

KEEPING THE CREW HAPPY

The Challenge: Keep a talented, creative in-house staff working on exciting, innovative projects rather than legacy systems maintenance.

The Solution: Have your Indian partner take over legacy systems support and maintenance.

Segmenting work between mission critical (but relatively boring) projects and "cool" leading-edge work enables companies to match the work done in-house to fit their talent profile. In addition, they can send the legacy maintenance or non-mission critical work offshore. Indian programmers are happy to work on projects that many talented U.S.-based in-house programmers dislike. Indian programmers regard work on legacy systems maintenance as a career opportunity and give it the attention it deserves. Indian developers aspire to work on more challenging projects, of course, just like their U.S. counterparts. But they understand the need to pay their dues with legacy maintenance work. Such projects, quite literally, give them a passport to global opportunities.

Not only does this approach help alleviate what can be a significant human resources management problem; at the same time it also drives overall costs lower. During my last trip home to India, I met a young man in a coffee shop. That meeting illustrates my point.

Sanjeev is working on a project to migrate legacy applications for a large American insurance company. I asked him how he liked this work. He smiled and said it wasn't exactly his dream job, although he likes working in technology. Nevertheless, he goes to work early and stays late because he understands that there is old and new in everything. "As a professional," he said, "I must master both if I am to deliver value in either."

I was so impressed I grabbed my pad and scribbled down his comments. It isn't everyday that you encounter such an insightful young IT professional. Sanjeev recognizes that the skills he learns today provide a foundation for him to migrate his career to more challenging skill sets, even as he works to migrate his client's legacy software.

BUILDING YOUR BULLPEN

The Challenge:	Have access to a well-trained group of specialists without having talented people sitting idle until you need them.
The Solution:	Let Indian firms provide a full range of technical specialists, when needed.

In many ways, a well-staffed IT department resembles a baseball team. To succeed throughout the season, the general manager must keep a lot of pitchers on the team with different styles or capabilities. Some are starters, some are mid-inning relievers, some are lefties, and at least one is a closer. That means a baseball team must carry a heavy payroll of pitchers. More often than not, most of these pitchers simply sit and watch the game like any other spectator. A CIO's staffing budget is hardly the size of the New York Yankees . . . or even the Texas Rangers. Most CIOs simply cannot afford to have talented, well-paid staff sitting in the bullpen.

Having rapid access to a wide range of detailed expertise can be enormously important when you have a problem in the myriad software, database and middleware systems you operate. It can make the difference between a rapid response and a long delay while waiting for a vendor expert. Worse yet, the problem may involve software interactions rather than an individual piece of software, making vendor troubleshooting a nightmare.

In contrast, the Indian partner can maintain a bench. It has a utilization rate of around 70 percent, so it has sufficient capacity to have available specialists in various platforms, tools, and technologies. Also, the Indian partner is typically vendor-neutral. Most importantly, there is a good chance your Indian partner has seen your problem before.

Your partner doesn't restrict itself to the products of any one particular company. For example, if you need middleware expertise, your Indian partner will have access to people trained on iPlanet, WebSphere, WebLogic, MQSeries, Biztalk, Vitria, or Tibco. The choice is yours. Therefore, it's easy to see the benefits of using an Indian partner to build your bench.

KEEP THE LIGHTS BURNING

The Challenge: Operate your IT network 24x7.

The Solution: Leverage your Indian partner's capability to deliver high quality software and knowledge of the latest system architecture developments.

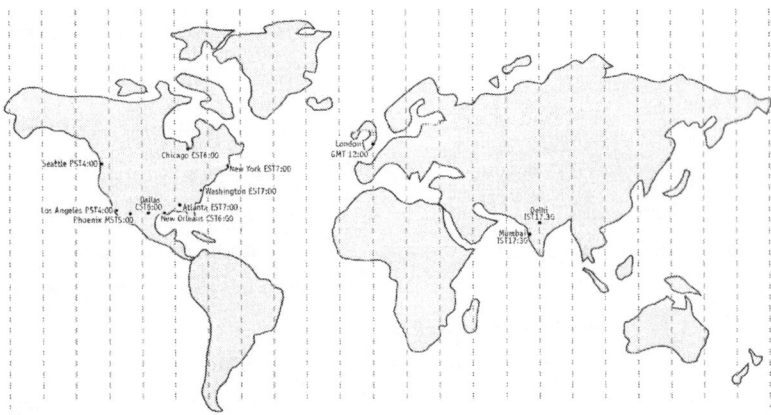

Graphic #13: Anytime Development – Working around the clock around the world

Your company's IT infrastructure must be up and running around the clock. In today's online, Web-based world systems must be available 24x7. The online terminal, customer service centers, and Websites are where your customers meet the business.

Indian firms maintain detailed knowledge of the newest hardware and architectural methods. They have serious R&D programs – backed with extensive relationships with top software vendors – allowing them to meet the accessibility/availability issues.

Indian firms can re-architect solutions for 24x7 environments . . . and then run operations support around the clock. In the knowledge business, running the graveyard shift is difficult. This is true even in India since programmers dislike being viewed as factory workers. That being said, however, the chances of a reliable three-shift operation are higher in India.

With an Indian partner, you also can create a virtual 24-hour workday by using teams and resources in sites distributed across the globe. Your U.S.-based team hands the work over to another team halfway around the world. It may be the end of the U.S. team's workday, but it's the beginning of the day in India. This approach creates a round-the-clock development environment, significantly reducing the time to delivery. Working together, much like a relay team, you can provide 24x7 coverage for IT support or call centers, or finish IT development projects faster.

It's little wonder, then, that execution using global resources has become popular for delivering both engineering and services projects. People often think such distributed projects require more work to implement successfully than projects based on the traditional approach. The reality is that with advance planning and attention to detail the distributed approach works better.

Here's why.

Perfect coordination is the key to successfully executing the onsite/offshore model. Ad hoc procedures may be all too common in the traditional, single location project model, but they are strictly off limits with an offshore approach. Everything has to be systemized. Everything has to be documented. This demand for constant discipline has a happy consequence. Your organization necessarily falls into a rigorous engineering groove. Put together, this ensures you have an IT infrastructure that rarely – if ever – fails and skilled people watching over your systems night and day.

Two Heads Are Better Than One

The Challenge: Have a strategic view of the IT system and new products and services.

The Solution: Bring your Indian partner in at the beginning, as part of the strategic planning process to apply the IT knowledge gained from your partner's R&D investments.

Today's CIO is under pressure to be a corporate thought leader, providing strategic insights and pressing for innovation in products and services, delivery, and infrastructure. The CIO is called on for strategic advice and innovation from developing new products to keeping ahead of the competition with new services, geographic expansion, and new markets. Falling behind on technology – whether in systems architecture, terminals, use of the Web, or new application software – puts the business in a precarious position, vulnerable to competitors who can move faster in adopting new improvements.

There are countless business stories about small competitors entering a market based solely on their new technology. A case in point is the impact that online brokerages have had on the old-line brokerage companies. It is the job of the CIO to guard against this kind of threat. And even today, the CIOs of old-line brokerage companies are scrambling to catch up with their newer, more nimble competitors.

Indian companies can be very innovative, helping the client CIO develop and implement strategies to leap ahead of the competition. Indian partners can also implement strategic initiatives quickly and affordably, reducing the risks inherent in innovation. Many CIOs leverage these investments as a strategic ace in the hole, "mining" their offshore partner as a source of ideas and innovation. Innovative CIOs use offshore providers (sometimes vendors, sometimes their own units) to spur technology enhancement, develop new products, gain access to new markets, and grow globally.

Let me give an example. We're all aware of companies that invested heavily in CRM solutions only to find their staff use the new systems sparingly and inconsistently. The returns on such investments are poor and it's hard to justify their costs.

That was the situation facing one leading Asian insurance company. Insurance agents in the field needed to update significant amounts of data about their customers during and after a meeting. Customer and policy data were supposed to be captured online. Most agents, however, found the process cumbersome and were less than happy with the time and effort it took them to make up a quote.

Mastek was asked to come up with a better solution – one that agents would actually be happy to use. Our company studied the problem and came up with an inexpensive and viable alternative to laptops and desk PCs. The solution was based on PDAs running full-fledged applications. Mastek architects designed an algorithm that compressed data into bite-sized chunks. What previously took up to 150 Mb on a desktop application required just 3 to 5 Mb on the PDA. Agents in the field could now carry in a pocket the huge database of information needed to calculate a client's premium.

Whenever the insurance company made changes in its rates, it could update this information for all its agents in seconds. Agents no longer needed to use a wire line to synchronize data. The data were simply uploaded onto the main system, the underwriter saw it immediately, and agents in the field received the correct, updated quote. This solution improved both the performance and morale of the sales force.

Another good example is the Lex Vehicle Leasing Company, one of the largest fleet leasing companies in the U.K. The company turned to Mastek to help it replace a legacy information system. As we developed an understanding of Lex's business of leasing vehicles to companies, we realized how to build in new strategic advantages for the company while replacing the legacy system. This primarily involved providing a service-call registration system, allowing customers to log and update vehicle service requests, and track the status of a vehicle from a mobile telephone.

As these examples demonstrate, Indian firms aren't just an opportunity to reduce expenses. Working as partners with the client company, these firms can help develop new products and channels. They can provide better integration, help mine data, and assist the client in building both better IT and business processes.

WE CAN DO MORE THAN THAT

The Challenge: Add value to the project – not just write code.

The Solution: Use your Indian partner's knowledge of your industry not only to develop software but also to provide complete solutions, from software to hardware ... to new business models.

To date, offshore outsourcing has concentrated on a relatively few industries. This concentration has allowed Indian outsourcing firms to drill down in these industries, developing a broad, deep understanding of the issues involved.

I recently read a news account by Arun Shourie, a journalist and now a minister in the government, of the metamorphosis of the old Long Term Credit Bank of Japan. Since 1952, LTCB was one of the principal financiers of Japan's phenomenal industrialization. By the 1990s, however, the bank was in trouble. Its troubles deepened to the point that the bank was forced to file bankruptcy. Despite every effort – including nationalization by the government – the bank continued to hemorrhage money. The inevitable result soon followed. To the horror of every Japanese, the bank was sold to foreigners and renamed the Shinsei Bank.

Now, just a few years later, the bank is back on its feet while other Japanese banks continue to struggle. Don't look in Tokyo for the reason for its success and others' failure. Look to India, where a thousand young professionals from a consortium of three firms transformed the bank and reorganized its operations around a completely new, modern business model.

Working in partnership with Shinsei Bank, the Indian consortium helped create a butterfly from a caterpillar, in record time and at a very affordable price. The new, transformed retail bank was launched within one year rather than the expected three. Costs for the project were 90 percent less than projected. A range of new financial products – better than what competitors offer – were launched. In addition, the bank's hardware infrastructure was downsized.

Any number of experienced IT professionals would be qualified to write the software needed to modernize the bank's systems. What made this transformation from bankruptcy to a competitive, thriving organization possible was that the Indian consortium could bring to bear expertise in a host of domains. They understood what needed to happen based on their past experience and knowledge of financial markets, modern commercial banking, and accounting practices. This deep, industry-specific understanding allowed the Indian consortium to provide not just software, but total solutions which support a new business model.

HOW DO YOU STAY IN CONTROL?

Challenge: Maintain in outsourcing offshore the same level of control the CIO has with on-site staff.

Solution: Control through process, not proximity.

Control is a priority for any CIO. When the possibility of working with an offshore vendor is discussed, a typical CIO might think: "It's hard enough to control the programmers down the hall. How can I maintain control over a project taking place halfway around the world?" After all, it's their neck on the line.

Many American CIOs strongly believe that a U.S.-centric model is essential for their company. They make passionate arguments for keeping their IT work in-house or at least in-country. Time and again, the main reason cited in support of this business model is the need for close oversight of the workforce.

In many ways, maintaining control of an offshore project is the same as maintaining control of an in-house project. Yet, it is quite different in other important respects. As with any project, having clearly defined work processes and documentation is critically important. These procedures must be worked out and agreed to by the client and its Indian partner at the outset of the program, and the documented processes must then be followed diligently by both parties.

Section 5 of this book describes the Governance and Management structures needed to perform designated functions through the entire program. This is crucial to the success of any offshore program. Regular, in-depth program reviews must be a part of the Governance structure.

The infrastructure underlying the program – including hardware and software – must be managed both at the client's location and at the partner's location. The infrastructure must support all of the development work being done at both locations, and it must support transfer of software between locations. Obviously, the infrastructure must operate 24x7 with very high availability. The importance of this task means that there must be an *Infrastructure Manager* on the team reporting to the Program Manager. We will deal with the infrastructure choices in more detail in Section 5.

This approach differs very little from the management rules typical of most IT organization. The differences begin to show up when dealing with the need to measure project progress accurately. As described later in the book, a Web-based tool must be put in place that enables all project managers to see daily reports of progress, expenditures, and error rates.

The single most important factor in maintaining control of an offshore project is for the client CIO to bring his team up to speed as quickly as possible to be able to manage the entire project. To do this, the CIO must implement a combination of formal education combined with on-the-job training. The requirement to train staff and put them in control of the project must be spelled out in the contract. Your partner is responsible for developing and administering the formal training program. The contract must set clear goals to transfer project control to your staff by a specific date.

These principles sound straightforward, and they are. Success comes from rigid adherence to every element discussed here. If you follow these principles, you will find yourself in a comfortable position of control throughout the project's life cycle.

There are some important steps you can take to maintain tight control of the offshoring process, including:

- Use your offshore partner to train your staff in managing an offshore program. After all, the people you will be working with have considerable experience in this area . . . put it to work for you.
- Approach the project committed to being true partners in program management. Set up a one-to-one relationship between

members of your management and governance teams and the corresponding members of the partner's team.

· Use the measurements made by your Indian partner's CMM shop to closely track progress. You can monitor their progress using the Web to view this data on a daily basis. Maintaining a strong, well documented process to manage and control the entire process gives your team confidence that they know exactly what work is being done.

After watching this process repeat itself again and again, one thing is clear. The better the client CIO manages the relationship with the Indian partner, the better the client's on-site staff becomes at executing this new business model.

So, Where Do You Go From Here?

Today, an American or European company can enter into a partnership with an Indian IT firm with confidence. U.S.-based IT managers can have peace of mind that projects will be delivered on time, on budget, and on target. Given the potential for significant cost savings and the high quality of the work delivered, it's incumbent upon IT managers to at least explore the possibilities.

Offshoring is moving beyond the exclusive domain of *Fortune 500* corporations. In increasing numbers mid-sized companies across America are exploring, and acting on, the many opportunities that offshoring presents in cost savings and revenue growth.

The cost of offshoring has also been driven down by the growing experience of American and Indian firms working together. This experience results in increased comfort levels with business processes between American clients and their Indian partners.

As a result of early experiences, many companies that only put their toe in the offshore waters have become believers. As in any courtship, the challenge today is to move the relationship to a higher level so IT managers view their Indian vendors more readily as strategic partners.

For many people the simple question is, Why India? For many Americans, including business leaders, India is something of a mystery. For some people, India is the land of Rudyard Kipling stories from childhood memories. But India is far more. It is the solution to a complex set of challenges facing many U.S. corporations today. In the next section, this book takes a detailed look at why India has become that solution.

SECTION FOUR

WHY INDIA

"Long years ago we made a tryst with destiny, and now the time comes when we shall redeem our pledge, not wholly or in full measure, but very substantially. A moment comes, which comes but rarely in history, when we step out from the old to the new, when an age ends, and when the soul of a nation, long suppressed, finds utterance."

—Jawaharlal Nehru*

BUILDING MOMENTUM

Jack Welch, renowned former CEO of General Electric, discovered India in 1989. GE's decision to outsource much of its technology work to India lacks the historical sweep of Columbus' adventures in the New World or Marco Polo's travels to China. Nevertheless, GE's move spawned a new era of business opportunities and innovation around the world. Only now is the full impact of GE's innovation being felt.

Welch saw a cost-effective source for software development in India.

---

*Speech in the Constituent Assembly, on the eve of India's Independence, August 14, 1947

He wrote in his autobiography, *Jack*, "The scientific and technical talent in India to do software development and basic research is incredible."

Legend has it that GE's love affair with India began when an Indian employee organized a speech by a visiting professor from an Indian technical school in the early 1990s. That talk in Schenectady, New York led to a research relationship between GE and the technical school. That relationship led GE to explore the advantages of setting up a research and development center in India.

GE moved into India slowly, but surely, partnering with several Indian vendors to outsource software development. GE now accounts for more than 8 percent of the total software exports of the Indian IT industry, outsourcing about $500 million in software development to India.

GE adopted what it called the 70-70-70 rule to guide its outsourcing initiatives worldwide. Under this guideline, about 70 percent of the work carried out by GE is outsourced. In turn, 70 percent of the outsourced work is done by a list of preferred vendors, with 70 percent of these projects done at the vendor's premises, i.e. offshore.[1]

GE's decision revolutionized the outsourcing offshore business. GE and other early pioneers like Citigroup sent enough work and investment to develop India's fledgling entrepreneurial companies. It also gave Indian vendors the credibility needed to approach other global corporations with numerous American and European companies soon following GE's lead.

Graphic # 14

[1] JPMorgan Case Study – GE's India Offshoring Success (June 22, 2001)

"I don't know anyone who is smart enough to do all things well," Keith Hughes, former chairman of The Associates, told me recently. "Jack Welch put it this way: 'If someone can do IT development cheaper, faster, and better than we can, that allows us to use our dollars either to return it to the shareholders or to invest in people who build better jet engines or run financial services better'."

GE continues to push to leverage offshore technology resources under Jeffrey R. Immelt, Welch's successor as Chairman and CEO. Immelt is investing heavily in expanded research and development capabilities, including a new research center in Bangalore, India.[1]

LESS EXPENSIVE, HIGHER QUALITY, AND ON-TIME

Cheaper, faster, better – or as we prefer: less expensive, higher quality, and on-time delivery. These are the key reasons why companies outsource their work to a variety of countries, led by India.

Not everyone at GE embraced offshore outsourcing at the beginning. Shaun Coyne, now CIO of Toyota Financial Services, was an early skeptic at GE. Before joining GE, he had worked for several years at Citibank, so he has been enmeshed in the offshore outsourcing issue.

"I did not believe in the outsourcing model necessarily," Coyne said. "Working for a company like GE, you have no choice. Whether you want to believe it or not, it was basically dictated to you, and a lot of us went kicking and screaming, saying it will never work. Over time, I slowly began to change my mind in terms of the value of outsourcing. What made me a believer was coming to India, with a number of staff, and actually seeing that it indeed does work."

Since then Shaun has been an evangelist and industry leader who has succeeded because of his belief and approach of ensuring buy-in across all levels of the organization

Ideally, any CIO considering outsourcing should visit Mumbai to see the advantages of technology or business process offshoring first-hand. Building any new relationship requires a lot of time and effort, particularly a long-distance relationship. This chapter starts the journey while sparing you a transoceanic airline trip. It explains why offshore

---

[1] "GE Chief Is Charting His Own Strategy, Focusing on Technology," *Wall Street Journal*, September 23, 2003, page B1.

outsourcing makes good sense overall and why outsourcing to India makes particularly good sense.

As discussed in the last chapter, this is a very timely topic due to the tremendous pressure on senior management – from CEOs to CIOs – to cut costs, provide higher quality, and produce timely, measurable results. The pressure to innovate and be more nimble in a rapidly changing business environment also is intense.

India now supplies more than 70 percent of all offshore software to the U.S. An examination of other pioneers in this area – such as Texas Instruments and Hewlett-Packard – illustrates the evolution of the IT and business process outsourcing industries in India. This historical perspective is necessary to fully comprehend why India so dominates the field.

THE TEXAS INSTRUMENTS EXPERIENCE

Texas Instruments identified India almost 20 years ago as a land of exceptional promise in the development of integrated circuitry. Looking to expand its presence in Asia, TI came to India to be more competitive. Like GE, TI opened the door to developing a country.

In two decades, TI has progressed from an initial focus on Electronic Design Automation software systems for integrated circuit design to the design of 3G Wireless chipsets and the development of Wireless LAN chipsets.

Now with about 1,000 employees in India, TI is an integral part of the country's technology landscape. TI India's extensive university relations program includes relationships with 39 universities. Its 39 digital signal processing (DSP) labs train more than 1,500 students in undergraduate and post-graduate studies a year. It is a leader in promoting relationships with domestic Indian companies. Since 2001, the company has established relations with 40 Indian companies. These companies work under TI's third-party global program, which enables local companies to reach global customers through TI's marketing channels.

RADHA BASU'S STORY

Hewlett Packard (HP) also has an extensive footprint in India. HP's relationship with India began with Radha Basu, who brought her company to India.[1] Basu left south India as a teenager to pursue graduate studies in computer science at the University of Southern California in the early 1970s. She entered the Silicon Valley technology market, beginning a long career at HP. When Basu returned to India in the mid-1980s, the government asked her to establish one of the country's first foreign subsidiaries. She spent five years establishing HP's software development center in Bangalore before returning to the U.S.

The first HP office in India consisted of a telex machine on Basu's dining room table. For many years, she produced physical evidence of software exports for customs officials who did not understand how the satellite data link worked. Basu couldn't convince Indian customs agents that it was possible to export software without material evidence. For five years she dumped systems data onto tapes and physically shipped them to U.S. customers so they could be registered and recorded as exports!

The situation improved drastically over time. Software Technology Parks with the latest in advanced communications and networking equipment dot the country. While other challenges remain – which we'll explore later in this book – the fact remains that momentum is building for offshoring to India.

OTHER PIONEERS

These pioneering companies are hardly alone in their interest in Indian outsourcing. According to a recent survey by Nasscom, about 82 percent of U.S. companies ranked India as their first choice for outsourcing research and development and software services. About 75 percent of the top 40 global IT services companies consider India to be country where they can locate research and development.

---

[1] From 'The Bangalore Boom: From Brain Drain to Brain Circulation?' by AnnaLee Saxenian, University of California at Berkeley

IBM Global Services is building its own development center in Bangalore and is increasing the number of software professionals it employs in India from 2,200 to 6,500 by 2004. "Virtually every global IT major is rapidly expanding its footprint into India," says Sunil Mehta, vice president of Nasscom.

EDS, for example, is increasing the number of people in its software development centers in India from 600 employees currently to 5,000. Microsoft's largest development center outside the U.S. is in India. More than 500 software professionals work at Microsoft offices in Bangalore and Hyderabad. Microsoft says it is moving strategic product related work to India to take advantage of the country's vast army of software developers.

Cisco, the global networking giant, has about 2,500 people working on projects in India and has told its Indian vendors to ramp up for more development work. Cisco has filed about 50 patents from India, an indication of the strategic value it's gaining from working in India. "India for us is an extension of our development community in Redwood Shores," said a senior Oracle official recently, referring to the software giant's Silicon Valley headquarters.

Many other U.S. and international companies share the feeling.

The Indian IT industry was in the right place at the right time. Beginning in the late 1990s, it captured the increased demand for IT services created by strong economic conditions, a growing dependence on technology solutions, and specific technological challenges, such as Y2K and e-commerce.

The growth of IT-enabled services is even more dramatic. This relatively new industry in India has grown 100 percent in the last five years and employs more than 100,000 people. McKinsey reports that ITES will reach $21 to $24 billion by 2008. Indian IT and ITES exports currently represent 20 percent of all foreign exchange. That is expected to grow to more than 30 percent of foreign exchange in 2008.

ADVANTAGE INDIA

India has what companies are looking for in an offshore vendor for information technologies: highly skilled software engineers who – due to favorable economic conditions in the country – are happy to work for wage scales well below their counterparts in the U.S., Ireland, or Canada.

According to The Gartner Group, India's pre-eminence is based on several factors, including:

- The visionary role played by the Indian government in promoting the software export industry
- Wide-spread fluency in English
- The large number of engineering graduates
- The Indian IT industry's drive for world-class quality

To be sure, the sort of success India enjoys doesn't just happen overnight. To put things in context, we need to explore some of the underlying reasons for this success.

NURTURING HANDS

Thankfully, in the 1990s the Indian government reversed years of repressive economic policies and began assisting the country's fledgling IT software export industry. Assistance took a variety of forms, including tax incentives for embryonic companies and lower tariffs, which reduced operating costs on computers and software. The government also built several software industrial parks that allowed these companies to house expensive computer systems and to attract college graduates to work there. In addition, investment in telecommunications infrastructure allowed Indian firms to export their software more easily and at lower cost.

Two Indian government officials, in particular, helped nurture the IT profession beyond its startup phase. Dr. N. Seshagiri designed the nation's Computer Policy of 1984, making it much easier to import computers. N. Vittal, Secretary for the Department of Electronics, introduced reforms that speeded up the governmental decision-making process. More importantly, he realized that India needed an inexpensive satellite data communication system – plus easy access to world-class technology, lower tariffs, and more IT professionals. Vittal created the Software Technology Parks of India, an innovation which provided advanced satellite data communication centers at affordable prices. These centers became incubators for emerging software companies.

In 1987, at the urging of Indian IT entrepreneurs, the government began opening technology to trade. Through Nasscom, founders of start-up IT companies pressed the government to reduce tariffs, which were then a staggering 110 percent. The government finally agreed and eliminated the tariffs altogether – dropping the duties to zero. That meant SAP enterprise software – which had cost twice as much in India as in other countries – was suddenly affordable.

Computer hardware makers in India took a different path. Indian manufacturers wanted to keep tariffs high in the belief that this would foster a domestic hardware industry. They succeeded in maintaining tariffs and today Indian manufacturers can even build supercomputer-class systems. Yet the industry never developed a significant market position in hardware sales.

Indian telecommunications capabilities were woefully inadequate in 1991. Capacity to the U.S. and Europe needed to expand, but telecommunications was controlled by the government monopoly known as VSNL. Here, too, IT entrepreneurs lobbied the government, seeking both investments in infrastructure and an opening of the VSNL monopoly on telecommunications. Telecom was a key infrastructure that needed improvements.

To gain funding for needed infrastructure improvements, Vittal announced in 1991 at the Nasscom conference that the Indian software industry would grow to $400 million in revenues within two years.

"We were stunned at his projection," said Ashank Desai, Mastek's chairman, who was then a young leader in the growing IT evolution in India. "We didn't think we could come close to that number in such a short time. But Vittal said it was necessary to convince the government to invest heavily in the infrastructure we needed. Fortunately we more than exceeded that goal."

Despite early successes, significant issues still faced the young industry. For example, equities markets were restricted because the Controller of Capital Issues set the price for new stocks, and it failed to see the potential of software companies. Small software companies also faced a dearth of financing. Banks would not lend money to software companies since they had no tangible assets for collateral. As a result, software companies grew slowly.

The government stepped in to solve the problem with the equities market. It abolished the Controller of Capital Issues office and permitted companies to decide IPO prices in consultation with investment bankers. At the time, venture capital was unavailable to Indian companies. Today, the availability of venture capital is a key factor, helping companies grow more rapidly.

The Reserve Bank of India was at one time a major stumbling block. The Bank eased restrictions on hiring foreign marketing companies and establishing sales offices abroad. (Restrictions on foreign travel also were relaxed.) Today few controls exist and companies are able to operate much as their U.S. counterparts do.

Vittal, an unflagging crusader, also understood that India needed to market itself as a technology resource to the world. That marketing effort became a principal responsibility of Nasscom. Much of the credit for the success in marketing – developing and enhancing India's image as a source of IT and IT-enabled services – goes to Nasscom.

Even with these successes and rapidly growing momentum in the marketplace, much work remains for India, Inc. to become the powerhouse brand it deserves to be.

THE COMMON DENOMINATOR – ENGLISH

With nearly 200 million English speakers – which will grow to 300 million by the end of this decade – India is poised to become the largest English speaking country in the world. Few in the U.S. realize that English is the official language of India, a most important legacy of the British Empire.

Graphic #15: English, the Common Language – English language newspapers abound in India; speaking English is the doorway to socio-economic status

In India, English is the surest way to gain upward mobility in business. A simple definition of the middle class is anyone who speaks English. If an Indian speaks English well, he or she can work in tourism, call centers, or a business processing shop and aspire to earn wages higher than most of his or her counterparts.

There are 17 major regional languages in India. The most widely spoken language in India is Hindi, but English unites the country in many ways. Other common languages include Tamil and Bengali, offshoots of Sanskrit.

Every college graduate speaks English, making it much easier to work effectively with American and British corporations. In other countries, the costs and delays involved in translating operating manuals from English to Chinese or other languages slows down the integration process significantly for vendors without a critical mass of English-speaking employees. Language differences with Chinese, Vietnamese, or Russians also complicate managing projects from the U.S.

HIGHER EDUCATION

China and India have very different strengths in education. China trains the masses in basic education well. India does not.

What India is very good at is higher education. Its institutions train graduates on par with the best in the world. That means the divide between the masses and the educated is wide.

India today has 256 universities and equivalent institutions, including 116 general universities, 12 science and technology universities, 7 open universities, 33 agricultural universities, 5 women's universities, 11 language universities, and 11 medical universities. There are universities focusing on journalism, law, fine arts, social work, planning and architecture, to name the major ones.

In addition, there are 10,750 colleges, which account for 80 percent of undergraduate and 50 percent of postgraduate education. There are 8 million students enrolled in Indian higher education, which has 400,000 teachers, making it the second largest educational system in the world.

The Indian Institutes of Technology (IIT) and the Indian Institutes of Management (IIM) form the centerpiece of this formidable system of higher education. These institutes rank among the world's finest centers of academic excellence.

Some of the most prominent chief executives, presidents, entrepreneurs, and inventors in the world are graduates of IIT, India's elite institution of higher learning. Its high standards, which compel the mostly male student body to average fewer than five hours of sleep a night, produce graduates who are masters at problem solving.

Getting into the Indian Institute of Technology, though, almost resembles qualifying for the Olympics. Leslie Stahl of the CBS News program *60 Minutes* said, "We discovered (that) IIT students consider themselves the luckiest people in India."

That isn't surprising, considering the competition for admission. First, there's the screening test held each December. Students who pass the screening test then take the Joint Entrance Examination, a grueling six-hour test in math, physics, and chemistry. Last year, almost 180,000 high school seniors took the entrance exam. Just over 3,500 were accepted – less than 2 percent. By comparison, Harvard accepts about 10 percent of its applicants.

Harvard, Princeton and MIT Combined

In India, IIT is as much a household name as Harvard is in the U.S. Or as Leslie Stahl put it: "Put Harvard, MIT, and Princeton together, and you begin to get an idea of the status of IIT in India. IIT is dedicated to producing world-class chemical, electrical, and computer engineers with a curriculum that may be the most rigorous in the world."

Indians make no secret of the almost athletic rigor schoolchildren undergo for the IIT exam. Tutoring and prep courses – called "coaching" – are par for the course, and the process begins as early as age three.

"In my family, nobody came to IIT before me. A lot of my friends and relatives tried," says Abhay Kumar Singh, 21, a student in his last year at IIT. "I was the only person who got in, so they are really proud." Half the battle may be getting in, but succeeding in IIT's hyper-competitive environment also is grueling. Singh says for most of his four years at IIT, he awoke at 7 a.m. and didn't fall asleep until 2 a.m.

"It's a tough life," said Singh, the lone student in the campus recreation center on a recent afternoon. No wonder, then, that an IIT degree today increasingly serves as a stamp of approval and provides credibility the world over.

Illustrious Alumni

While IIT produced talented engineers, scientists, and managers for four decades, the school is recently gaining worldwide recognition largely because of some of its prominent alumni. Among the senior level executives in American corporations who trace their lineage to the halls of IIT are Victor Menezes, Citigroup; Rakesh Gangwal, US Airways; Rajat Gupta, McKinsey & Co.; and Vinod Khosla, the co-founder of Sun Microsystems, Inc. Hundreds of other Indians work in the top ranks of U.S. corporations and technology powerhouses in Silicon Valley. In fact, four out of 10 Silicon Valley startups are run by Indians.

Many Wall Street firms rely on IIT graduates to devise the complex algorithms behind their derivatives strategies, while big multinationals call on them to solve problems in new ways. When recruiting from colleges for its consultant ranks, McKinsey hires a significant number of the school's graduates every year. Many more write the software and design the chips and peripherals that Silicon Valley sells to the world.

The rise of IITians, as they are known, is a telling example of today's global capitalism. And, while IIT is now the best known, many other fine institutes have exported talent that has helped build the India Inc. brand. My own alma mater, St. Stephen's College has consistently produced ambassadors for India in every field – some of whom I have had the pleasure of knowing, include the Rhodes Scholar and career diplomat, Aftab Seth; the UN wunderkind and author Shashi Tharoor, the former CEO of Standard Chartered Bank, Rana Talwar; a long time director of McKinsey, Tino Puri; and a rising star at Citi today, Ajay Banga. They and the thousands of other Indians that you encounter everyday have made the global citizen possible. A highly-educated, intensely ambitious college graduate making his or her way in the world, seeking a challenging career, even if it is thousands of miles from home.

What is it about the Indian student that programs him to vault to Olympian heights in science and technology? To answer this intriguing question, we need to understand India's quantitative orientation and the rigor of its educational system.

A LOVE AFFAIR WITH MATHEMATICS

India enjoys a rich and ancient heritage in mathematics. The ancient Indians' most celebrated achievements in mathematics include:

- Developing the concept of zero (mentioned in Pangala, Chandra Sutra 200 AD)
- Developing the decimal place notation (references dating back to 100 BC)
- Algebra was known in India centuries before it spread to Europe
- Aryabhatta, a 5th century B.C. mathematician, proved the Pythagorean theorem long before Pythagoras was born

(Baudhayana, Baudhayana Sulba Sutra, 600 BC, 1000 years before Pythagoras)

- Calculating the time taken by the earth to orbit the sun at 365.258756484 days (Bhaskaracharya, Surya Siddhanta 400-500 AD)

In modern India, mathematics assumes even greater importance given its role in shaping careers. Without superior skills in mathematics, few students in India go very far. In India, the dream of practically every bright student is to forge an engineering career. To achieve this dream, a student must master the most intricate aspects of mathematics. Consider the following facts about India:

Forms of ZERO

Graphic #16: Evolution of 'Zero'

- Children are taught to count practically from the day they can speak.
- Numbers are held in such high esteem that parents coax, cajole, and threaten in efforts to ensure their children learn their multiplication tables.
- A student's brilliance in mathematics is celebrated at school, at home, and among peers. A mathematically gifted boy – far from being labeled a *nerd* or a *geek* – is accorded the same status as a football player in America.
- Numerology is an integral part of religions in India. The significance and symbolism of numbers is celebrated and deified.

Asian students in general, and Indians in particular, typically outperform their U.S. counterparts on international comparisons of mathematical competency. Many surveys establish the fact that American secondary school students compare poorly on tests of mathematical achievement with students from many other countries, but especially with students from Asia.

Students in India spend a great deal more time in mathematics class than do American students. School is in session 240 days per year in India, but only 200 days a year in the U.S. Fifth-grade students in Mumbai attend school 44 hours per week. In most U.S. schools, they spend 30 hours per week.

India remains a nation of people bound to the magic of numbers. In many ways, the country's growing success in the high technology industry is only a footnote in its never-ending journey to numerical nirvana.

The Sanctity of Grades/Scores

Indian professionals are fixated on their class rank. An Indian graduate's college rankings stay with him or her for life. When an Indian professional meets a former classmate, it is common and expected for each to remember what ranking the other had in the class. Class reunions are difficult for those who ranked low.

Best selling author Michael Lewis, in his book The New New Thing, writes about the IIT graduates whom Jim Clark (the founder of Silicon Graphics, Netscape and WebMD) sought out: "they were ferociously, recklessly competitive. Pavan and Kittu had finished in the top one hundredth of one percent on the test taken by bright young Indians who probably were already in the top one-hundredth of one percent on the national brainpower scale. Yet about twice a week, Pavan found a way to remind Kittu that he had finished 250 places behind him."

COMMITMENT TO QUALITY

Initially, Indian companies competed exclusively on low price, the result of cheap labor. But most top companies now seek higher levels of quality. This shows in many areas. Some companies, like Mastek, replace all their computers every two years. We may not replace the carpet, but our developers have the best tools.

Of the top 300 Indian software companies, 170 are ISO certified. Worldwide, there are only 74 companies that have achieved CMM Level 5 certification. Of those, 50 are located in India.

Warren Gallant, president and vice chairman of Technology Partners International (TPI), the world's leading outsourcing advisory firm, points out: "U.S. companies want to come to India because of the quality of the work. In India the time to market is low and you have the flexibility to scale up the high quality resources as per your requirements."

The passion for quality is a reflection of India itself: a paradoxical phenomenon. In ancient times the quality of Indian exports – including spices, handicrafts, gems, and the arts – were exceptional. More recently, however, the quality of manufactured goods has been spotty.

The technology industry is a throwback to the best of Indian traditions, although the reason remains unclear. Unlike manufacturing, IT involves fewer logistics issues and, therefore, fewer potential points of failure. But the most interesting subliminal reason may be that the Brahmins, the priestly caste at the helm of the Indian IT industry, view their businesses as their calling and approach it with the same fervor for quality as their ancestors had for the scriptures and music.

INDIAN WORK ETHIC

Indians tend to be angular, not well rounded. Few Indians have hobbies. With few avocations to keep them busy, most Indians immerse themselves in work, quite often blurring the lines between office and home.

Clearly these are generalizations. But they do apply in large measure. The reasons can be traced to the fact that the country is relatively poor – a powerful reason to stay focused. In addition, India is the cultural birthplace of yoga, which stands for a single-minded focus of the 'four stages' of life (learner, householder, coach, and ascetic), which again focus the karma or actions on the present stage.

For all these reasons, long hours at work are seen as a badge of honor. When foreign buyers visit, it is not seen as a reason to party (as in some cultures), but a reason to rededicate themselves, to get more and more interesting work, to come closer to the customer.

THE BEST PARTY IN TOWN

The IT profession is the pinnacle of careers in India. It attracts the best and brightest students. In the U.S. and Europe, the best and brightest students have a wide selection of choice jobs. IT is a good job in the U.S., but it does not pay as well as some other professions (i.e., law, accounting). As a result, U.S. companies realize they can have the best and brightest India has to offer. In India, an IT professional can expect three to five times the compensation of graduates in any other field.

Maybe the best analogy I can think of is sports. In America the best athletes play football, basketball, or baseball because these sports get the most attention. As professionals, athletes in these sports command the most fans – and the biggest salaries. In colleges, school resources go to fund the big three sports, often leaving other sports to fight for scraps.

In India, technology is the equivalent of football, basketball, and baseball rolled into one. It is far and away the best, most lucrative game in town. As a result, it attracts the brightest graduates.

HOW IT ALL BEGAN

India did not become a powerhouse in the IT world overnight. The Indian IT industry is very young – much younger than the world IT industry. It evolved quickly from the introduction of the first computer, an IBM 1620. Today, many of the largest, most successful companies in the world turn to Indian technology companies for solutions to complex problems. Indian IT companies provide innovative answers to strategic questions that have vexed businesses and governments for decades, if not generations.

Getting to this point in the development of India's technology industry demanded that a handful of IT entrepreneurs travel a very tough road. They had to take on not only the challenges presented by a large, insular country, but also a parochial global community, which saw India as a stagnant former British colony rather than a vibrant developing country.

Starting in the 1970s, there were only a handful of Indian IT companies whose first priority was to ship software overseas. Over the past three decades, the IT industry has grown from 5 to 500 companies, and the work has evolved from "body shopping" to strategic partnerships that provide leverage to U.S. and European companies.

Today, Indians hold 45 percent of the H1-B visas issued by the U.S. each year. There are 3.2 million Indians living in the U.S.

THE FIRST STIRRINGS OF A TECHNOLOGY POWERHOUSE

In 1959, IBM installed its 1620 at the Indian Statistical Institute in Calcutta. Other educational institutions – IIT (Kanpur), the Tata Institute of Fundamental Research, and National Physical Laboratory – followed suit in buying the early computers, a factor that would have a significant effect on future generations.

Corporations, however, used computers only for rudimentary applications, such as payroll, inventory, and fixed-asset accounting. In the West, and even in some less developed economies, businesses were already employing more advanced computers – the IBM 360 and 370 series, for example.

The Indian government banned the importation of IBM computers because it wanted to protect the government-owned Electronics Corporation of India, Ltd. (ECIL), which was producing mini-computer hardware. ECIL's hardware showed promise, but the company could not develop the software needed to maximize the potential of the machines. As a result, Indian corporations and institutions had access only to outdated and expensive imported technology – or inadequate domestic systems. The Indian government even controlled what computers Indian corporations could purchase or what spare parts could be imported.

Imported computer hardware was prohibitively expensive due to government-imposed duties of up to 150 percent. The government further required that many computer components be manufactured in India. That might have helped, if Indian companies were able to manufacture hardware components at the time.

Obviously, this was no foundation on which to build a powerhouse IT industry.

"The lack of access to computing equipment was one of the reasons why India lost a great opportunity to be on a par with China and the South-East Asian economies," wrote Infosys' chairman, Narayana Murthy, one of the pioneers of the Indian software industry.

The IBM Ouster – A Blessing in Disguise

In 1977, India expelled IBM and any other global companies that refused to dilute ownership of their Indian subsidiaries. This decision – which shocked the country and many in the IT industry worldwide – proved to be a blessing in disguise for the Indian IT industry. Between 1977 and 1989, India was forced to bring in smaller, cheaper, but often state-of-the-art minicomputers and microcomputers. Brands such as HP, Digital, Data General, PRIME, and Apollo were imported.

Indian companies also started using a nascent operating system (OS), UNIX, supplied by some of these vendors. One result is that many Indian IT professionals have worked with the popular UNIX OS longer than most other IT professionals.

Driven by information management requirements, the Indian government funded domestic IT development projects. This infusion of project capital cultivated India's IT industry, enabling it to blossom on its own. Mastek was a key player in some of these projects, helping itself and other young IT companies gain experience with these earliest software development projects.

During this period, Indian educational institutions expanded their IT curricula as colleges offered bachelor degrees in computer science education. Advanced degree programs in computer science launched in the early 1970s.

Developing the export market was the industry's key goal. India's relatively small domestic market – whether for corporate or government needs – was insufficient to keep a thriving industry busy. The Indian government gave the export effort a major boost by turning a negative into a positive. In the mid-1970s, the Mantosh Sondhi Committee, a Commerce Ministry group that oversaw the growth of India's engineering industries, allowed companies to import computer hardware if they agreed to export software. Companies could lease products from software export companies in return for imported hardware. Although problems occurred with this system, it funneled investment into software companies, focusing their attention beyond India's domestic market.

Scaling the Heights — By Paying Your Dues

Indian IT professionals needed to prove their mettle. In the early days of the country's IT development, the software development skills and experience of Indian professionals remained something of an open question. Clients often wanted to see Indian IT professionals work on-site at their offices to oversee their work closely. Also, the needed hardware and software wasn't available in India at the time to complete the work. As a result, Indian professionals worked on-site at client companies, rather than in India, in a practice known as "body shopping."

As Indian technology companies demonstrated their professional capabilities, corporations started outsourcing work directly to India. But, the process occurred over several years.

Unlike many other developing countries, Indians didn't migrate to escape persecution or famine. They left mainly to find work. In many cases, Indians followed their one-time colonial masters into the plantations of the West and East Indies and Africa, and later as entrepreneurs to most corners of the world.

Migration to the U.S. was spurred by President John Kennedy's goal to "put a man on the moon and return him safely to Earth." Droves of engineers and doctors seized the opportunities created in NASA and within university research labs and hospitals in the 1960s and 1970s. This led to the stereotype in the U.S. of Indians as medical or research professionals. From there, the image evolved into a broader view of the Indian as a technical professional, a logical progression. The work ethic of these industrious early immigrants made possible the subsequent growth in quantity and quality of people migrating to the U.S. from India.

Payoff Time – The Start of the Gold Rush

With rising exports and increasing foreign investments, the software industry's impact on India's economy is dramatic. The IT industry will increase from 1.4 percent of the Indian economy in 2001 to about 7 percent by 2008. By that time, the industry – which currently employs about one million people – will employ more than two million people directly. In addition, the indirect employment base will provide jobs for another two million people.

The $10 billion Indian IT industry is today very fragmented with the top five firms controlling approximately 30 percent of the market. The next 15 firms control another 20 percent. And the balance of the industry, nearly 600 firms, has about 50 percent. By 2010 when the IT industry is expected to reach $50 billion in size, this structure will undoubtedly have evolved significantly. While it is anyone's guess how the industry will evolve, I believe the progressive Indian firms – the majors, some mid-tier players, and even perhaps a firm not yet born, will garner 40 percent of the much expanded market. The global majors, which are largely on the sidelines at present, will rapidly pick up another 40 percent through organic and inorganic growth. And, since software is not scale dependant (although peace-of-mind may be) niche players will retain up to 20 percent, based on close relationships with select companies.

It will be an exciting rocket ride! For at least another 15 to 20 years. A Boston Consulting Group study estimates that by 2020 India will have 47 million surplus workers while most other nations will have a net deficit of workers. (China will absorb all the workers it produces for domestic needs). To grow the world's economy, and keep socio-economic calm in India, these surplus workers will be deployed as part of global teams, onsite and offshore.

Moving Up the Value Chain, One Step at a Time

The growth of India's IT industry is changing the world's perception of the country. India is clearly emerging as an important player on the world's technology stage.

What brought on this growth? How did India pull this off? To get a clearer picture of the evolutionary timeline, it is helpful to view the Indian IT and IT-enabled services industries in four distinct phases.

PHASE 1: EXPORTING PEOPLE

The first phase in developing India's IT industry was the "body shopping" era. IT companies exported trained IT professionals to other countries where they augmented growing corporate IT staffs. U.S. and European corporations imported Indian IT professionals either as employees or, in many cases, as contract labor. This approach reduced expenses by about a third. About 20 million Indians live overseas in a powerful Diaspora. Their combined income, estimated at $160 billion, is more than a third of India's GDP. They are a source of inspiration to many Indians.

Companies like GE, Texas Instruments, and Citibank took the initial steps toward outsourcing offshore in India. These companies established captive units in India, either in partnership with Indian companies or as stand-alone companies or divisions. Indian professionals developed a reputation for lower costs and hard work. As they joined the ranks of corporate IT departments they were assigned to fulfill relatively low-level tasks. India was the less expensive solution.

PHASE 2: EXPORTING LOW-END WORK — Y2K AND E-COMMERCE

In the 1990s, Y2K caused considerable fear in the corporate world and opened up opportunities for Indian firms to do more advanced projects. Some of today's largest Indian IT firms grew rapidly doing Y2K work. It was a breakthrough. U.S. and European companies discovered they could outsource projects directly to India and take advantage of both low cost and better processes. In this second phase, India was not only less expensive, it offered higher quality work.

PHASE 3: DEVELOPING 24x7 OPERATIONS

We've all heard that the three key factors in real estate are location, location, and location. This real estate cliché is also one of India's key strategic advantages. India's location halfway around the world – and more importantly 11-plus time zones removed – is a critical benefit for American customers.

The time zone differential means that Indians are awake and working while their American clients are asleep. Can you imagine a better strategic advantage? Throughout the day Indian professionals develop new programming which is then reviewed the same day in America.

This means projects move forward much more quickly. In addition, as we've discussed, Indians don't mind working long hours and, hence, are able to talk directly with their American counterparts at the beginning or end of the Indian workday. Indian companies rapidly developed the ability to provide 24x7 operations.

PHASE 4: OFFERING STRATEGIC PARTNERSHIPS

Indian companies are moving rapidly to become true strategic partners with their corporate clients. They are developing the ability to leverage their strategic advantages – cheaper, faster, and higher quality development, to create business leverage. That is, using their growing domain knowledge and architecture and development skills, Indian companies provide business solutions, not just technology fixes.

The future lies in partnering with Indian firms to produce marketplace advantages in which the Revenue to Expense ratio is 5:1 or 10:1 or more, as opposed to the first generation where a 50 percent reduction in costs (or a revenue-to-expense ratio of 2:1) was the goal.

Companies that come late to the offshore outsourcing game enjoy the very real benefits of avoiding Phases One, Two, and Three. Late entrants can leapfrog the early stages and go immediately to the strategic leverage stage. Indian firms, including my own company, currently work on projects at very advanced levels of business, government, and technology to provide strategic advantages.

Today, all four phases of evolution are still active as companies partner with Indian IT firms at varying levels of sophistication. However, the smart move is to skip the first three Phases and move immediately to Phase 4. This allows you to maximize leverage.

Simply put, if a U.S. company is going to deal with the issues involved in working in India – and they are not trivial – then it might as well strive to achieve the maximum advantage.

WHERE DO WE GO FROM HERE?

Indian companies are at a crossroads, brought on by their extraordinary success to date. The challenge for larger Indian IT companies is to compete successfully with the largest international consulting firms and major U.S. outsourcing companies. To compete effectively in this arena, Indian IT companies must expand services, build a world-class front-end, and open multi-national development centers.

Second-tier Indian firms must decide whether to compete with first-tier firms or concentrate on niche services.

Niche firms must maintain and expand the quality of their offerings to ensure that they continue to provide high-value services. This requires significant investment in technology and staff training. In addition, niche firms also must partner with other larger consulting firms – both within India and elsewhere.

Other than size, there is seemingly little to differentiate the various Indian IT firms. There are, however, important soft factors that differentiate the firms. And some firms are gaining market share by focusing on specific industries. Some will become global contract manufacturers. Others will be global systems integrators. A few will be narrowly focused providers. Fewer still will focus exclusively on research and development. The future, nonetheless, is exciting.

THE MOVE TO CALL CENTERS

Building on its success in the overall IT arena, India moved to establish some of the highest quality call centers in the world. Skilled, highly motivated English-speaking workers staff these call centers supported by the latest technology.

Indian IT-enabled services – telemarketing, help desk support, medical transcription, back-office accounting, payroll management, legal database management, and insurance claim and credit card processing – could reach half a trillion dollars by 2008.

Nasscom lists more than 200 IT-enabled service firms in its membership. The potential for expansion of these services is vast. The opportunity is driven by more competitive wages, higher motivation of the workers, and, of course, the ability of millions to speak English.

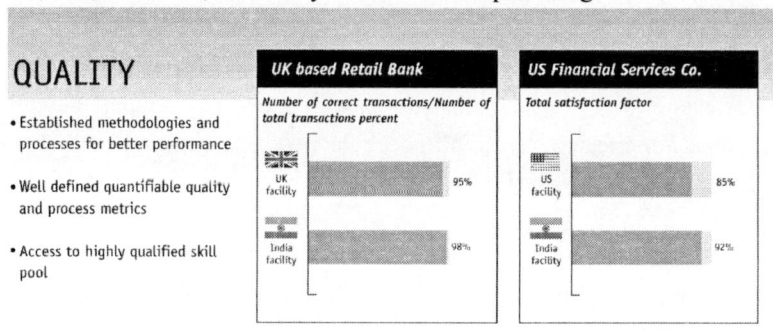

QUALITY

• Established methodologies and processes for better performance

• Well defined quantifiable quality and process metrics

• Access to highly qualified skill pool

UK based Retail Bank

Number of correct transactions/Number of total transactions percent

UK facility — 95%

India facility — 98%

US Financial Services Co.

Total satisfaction factor

US facility — 85%

India facility — 92%

Graphic #17: Quality in ITES

Help-desk work also plays to Indian cultural strengths – the inclination to be helpful. I recently heard of an off-beat use of Indian skills. A Phoenix-based psychiatric counseling service is exploring the possibility of employing Indians as counselors for American patients suffering from emotional problems and needing round-the-clock telephone access to a counselor. Indians make sympathetic listeners.

Entry-level call center workers in India receive about 10 to 15 percent of comparable U.S. or European salaries. While that seems low by the standards of a developed country, it's a higher wage than many other service sector jobs in India, and much higher than the national average.

While call center jobs in the U.S. and Europe are considered low-end jobs, with high turnover and absenteeism, in India they are considered high-quality employment. Turnover at Indian call centers is high, by comparison to IT firms. But that is primarily because call centers hire young people who are keen to move on to other, more challenging jobs.

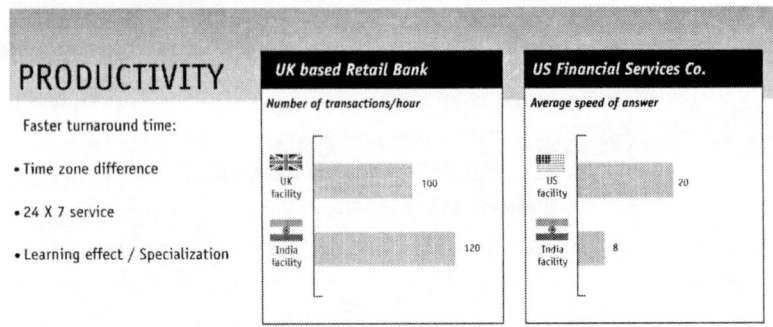

Graphic #18: Productivity in ITES

It is not unusual to see young Indian professionals camped in front of television sets watching old American TV shows like "Dallas" to work on their American accents and vocabulary. As we discussed earlier, in India, if you can speak English, it is virtually an automatic ticket to the middle class.

The Wall Street Journal reports that a London-based travel agency has taken outsourcing to a new level by shipping to India both the agency's call center positions and the workers who book the travel. The company, e-Bookers, is "pitching the job as a way to see the world, the information age equivalent of joining the Peace Corps or the Foreign Legion."[1]

The work environment for Indian call centers is also very attractive. The facilities are state of the art with multi-media communications infrastructures. These call centers have the latest networking and IT systems, combined with sophisticated power and telecommunications back-up systems. This enhanced support compensates for India's sometimes-inferior utilities.

The call center industry attracted some aggressive Indian entrepreneurs. Some of their firms will be highly successful. Others may fail or merge with thriving companies, as the Indian call center industry consolidates and matures.

TO HIGHER VALUE SERVICES

Development of the call center industry in India is something of a stepping stone to more complex and higher value IT and business process

---

[1] Wall Street Journal, October 13, 2003

outsourcing services. Without undervaluing their challenge, call centers are less complex than other business process tasks, such as Wall Street investment banking research, bank check processing, and even routine business legal work. These activities represent high-end, high-value services that open the door to longer-term, more strategic relationships between Western corporations and Indian firms.

For example, we recently launched a joint venture with Carreker Corporation, an expert in the software solutions business for financial service companies. The joint venture, called Carretek, addresses a growing challenge in the banking arena in transaction processing, fraud and research.

It is estimated that, over the next five years, U.S. banks will lose $900 million in revenues as a result of electronic payments and check conversions. U.S. banks must reduce their payment processing costs by $1.85 billion over the next several years just to keep up with declining revenues and escalating costs.

New technologies – including imaging technology to help bridge the paper and electronic conversions – will solve the problem. Thanks to image processing technology, we can perform the required payment functions in multiple locations with multiple systems. This lowers costs (e.g., less transportation), reduces risk (e.g., more fraud filters applied more quickly), and makes information available to a variety of paying parties.

Until very recently, payment processing through offshore outsourcing was difficult to justify. Today, half a dozen global financial institutions with their own facilities in India have begun processing payments offshore, including ABN AMRO, American Express, Cigna, Citibank, HSBC, and Standard Chartered. Carretek provides banks the high quality, lower cost solutions they require.

The potential for India in the area of higher value, strategic services is only now being realized. It is relatively small today, but in coming years it is likely to play a major role in the economic growth of India – and in strengthening the relationships between Indian firms and their American partners.

Geoffrey Colvin, a senior editor at *Fortune* magazine, raised the questions in a column he wrote in the fall of 2003, "What makes anyone think that progression is suddenly going to stop? The next rungs on the ladder (for India, China, and Philippines) are product innovation, brand building and overall management. We are looking at three billion people getting better by the day at the things that make us the world's leading economy."

Understanding India, Land of Contrasts

India is a nation rich in talent, yet burdened by poverty. This paradox constantly begs the question: "If you're so smart, how come you aren't rich?" To understand this puzzle, one must take a step back in time through India's history.

For every true statement you can make about India, the opposite also is true. India is poor, but some Indians are rich. The world's largest middle class – some 300 million people – is found in India. Yet the world's largest impoverished class – another 300 million people – is also found in India.

Downtown Mumbai to me is the square root of Manhattan in size, complete with skyscrapers, luxury hotels, and McDonald's fast food restaurants – with Maha Veggie Burgers instead of Big Macs. At the same time, many villages in India are dirt poor. The air is heavy with fumes of cow dung (used as fuel), homes that are little more than mud huts, and subsistence farmers at the mercy of the weather.

India is one of the most diverse countries in the world. Geographically it is the seventh largest country in the world, and second only to China in population. Stretching from the Himalayas to the tropical shores of the Indian Ocean, the country includes a vast number of languages, cultures, ethnic groups, religions, and lifestyles. It has some of the world's tallest mountains and 2,000 miles of coastline, a vast desert and the world's wettest spot. It is truly a subcontinent with as much diversity as Europe.

Your first visit to India attacks all your senses. It is a noisy country, frenetic at times, vibrant and seemingly chaotic. It is a land of contrasts and paradoxes. Serene beauty exists amid the chaos. Simultaneously India is both a very young nation – founded in 1947 – and a very old land. Recorded history in India goes back 5,000 years. Young and old frequently collide.

India is orthodox and rigid, yet highly creative. Its culture is heavily influenced by the influx of outsiders. There is no monolithic culture. Northern Indians are usually light skinned and naturally outgoing. Southerners tend to have darker skin and are more intellectual. The East has a strong tradition in literature and the arts, while the West is historically the trading center and is today quintessentially entrepreneurial.

India is a chrysalis . . . a caterpillar in transformation. It is a picture of contrasts and of a country in transformation.

The India You Never Knew

· Emperor Aurangzeb had 10 times the revenues of his French contemporary, King Louis XIV.

· In 1497, Vasco da Gama visited India and wrote about large cities, buildings, and jewels, prompting Christopher Columbus to sail off in search of a faster passage to the country. Tales of great riches in India also influenced the British, who sailed off in the opposite direction and actually got there.

· By 1914, India had the third largest railway network in the world, the largest jute manufacturing, fourth largest cotton production, biggest canal system, and 2.5 percent of the world trade.

· India developed a merchant class that was hungry for growth and a bureaucracy that thwarted growth.

· India is 124th among the nations of the world on a per capita basis. But its $478 billion GDP ranks as the 12th largest economy in the world with the second fastest growth rate. Optimistic projections show the country poised to be a $9 trillion power-house by 2020 on a PPP basis.

· India includes the world's largest concentration of poor and illiterate people, yet it graduates 500,000 engineering and technical students annually and another 2.5 million other graduates a year, more than any other country.

· India's 56-year-old political system, despite at-times para-lyzing political in – fighting, is the largest and one of the strongest democracies in the world. In the last national elec-tions, almost 400 million people cast ballots.

Mumbai and Bangalore — A Tale of Two Cities

Mumbai is home to some of the most important software development companies in India. Originally a collection of seven swampy islands, Mumbai is the commercial center of India.

Mumbai is a city of striking contrasts. Skyscrapers stand next to stately Victorian buildings. Bazaars compete with glittering new shopping malls for customers. Sprawling slums surround wealthy neighborhoods. The population of the city grows rapidly as people from all over India flock there in search of career opportunities.

Mumbai, originally founded by the Portuguese who named it Bombay, became part of the British Empire in 1661. Seeing little potential in the swampy islands on the Arabian Sea, the British government leased the islands for a pittance to the East India Company. The entrepreneurs of the East India Company quickly realized the importance of the natural harbor as a port and shipbuilding center. Bombay attracted a diverse population that continues to give the city a vibrant multicultural identity.

Bombay seems overbuilt and overcrowded, but it is not overrated. It remains the number one city for business with the best connections worldwide. It also has the best power and public infrastructure and an unparalleled work ethic, built around its heritage of commerce. While it does not have the space for lavish business campuses, it is the "City that Works."

Modern India – driven by cyber cafes, satellite television, and cellular telephones – produces rapid change in an old land. Nowhere is this change more visible than in the "Electronic City" of Bangalore in the heart of India's "Silicon Valley."

Bangalore is a large city located in the south of India. The climate is much gentler year-round than in Mumbai with more trees and greenery throughout the city. The population isn't as congested in the city, and the level of poverty isn't as visible. Bangalore developed over the past 15 years as the home of some of India's most prominent technology companies. Companies there produce computer hardware and software, distribute products worldwide, and conduct basic research and development.

Bangalore's "Electronic City" is headquarters for such national and multinational information technology companies as Oracle and Texas Instruments.

The corporate campuses of some technology companies in Bangalore look more like universities surrounded by five-star hotels, rather than a government-funded IT incubator.

Dignitaries and corporate executives are regular visitors to Bangalore. On one day recently Tom Engibous, chairman and CEO of Texas Instruments, and the President of Ukraine were in Electronic City on separate visits. The President of Russia and Microsoft chairman Bill Gates followed close on their heels.

Bangalore is enjoying a major growth spurt. The growth of India's technology sector requires improvements in everything from roads to apartments and town homes to new and expanding support businesses. The growth is attributed directly to the technology sector of the economy.

Graphic #19: Indian IT Centers

Other cities in India are growing handsomely and quite often challenge Mumbai and Bangalore in attracting new business. Each city is well entrenched in the technology race and is hungry to emulate the success of Mumbai and Bangalore. Among the most aggressive locations in India are:

- Hyderabad – City of Pearls
- Chennai – Gateway of Southern India
- Kochi – Queen of the Arabian Sea
- Kolkata – City of Joy
- Ahmedabad – Manchester of the East
- Pune – Queen of the Deccan
- Delhi, Noida and Gurgaon (NCR – National Capital Region) – The Capital City

The Historical Backdrop

India largely missed the industrial revolution. Today, India's economy ranks just 124th in the world, yet historically India was among the world's richest nations. It is a matter of much debate among economists, Indian nationalists, and the British intelligentsia why India missed the industrial revolution and fell so far behind countries it once was ahead of economically.

The opinions range from economic theories involving imperialist drain and fragmentation of agriculture to Hindu equilibrium and the enervating heat. The bottom line is that there was no investment in technology or the development of a lead sector for the economy to take-off.

The British did not loot India. But, neither did they invest in India at critical times. In 1947, when India became independent, 83 percent of all Indians were illiterate. Some 100,000 British bureaucrats ran India. They only managed the books. They did not know how to grow a country. The British Empire was founded by entrepreneurs, but managed by bureaucrats.

The Caste System

No discussion of India is complete without looking at the caste system. Indeed, it shapes the way Indians behave.

The much-abused caste system was a unique basis for maintaining peaceful coexistence. While it is officially abolished today, its influence is still felt in the popular psyche. The system started 3,000 years ago when neo-Aryans invaded the country and – instead of annihilating the native inhabitants – absorbed them by giving them a lower place in society.

In time, the structure developed into four tiers with Brahmins, who were teachers and priests, at the top, followed by Kshatriyas, who were the warriors and rulers, Vyshyas, who performed commercial operations, and Sudras, who did manual labor and farming. These classes were not rigid and depended as much on the natural state and physical being as on heritage.

Over the centuries, however, any flexibility disappeared and vicious undertones took over. Manual work, including agriculture, was disdained, leading to the appalling nomenclature "untouchables." Business people were only slightly better. Profit was a dirty word; bureaucrats did their best to leave little profit for the businessman, while the wily traders did their best to squeeze out as much profit as possible.

The typical civil servant grew up in a professional, salaried family and considered himself informed, educated, and "honest," looking down on the semi literate, tax-dodging, street-smart traders. (Of course, the traders' views of bureaucrats' honesty are another story!) With illiteracy rates at 80 percent and above, the upper classes – priests and teachers – had a vested interest in maintaining the status quo and used fate, reincarnation, and karma to subdue the aspirations of the masses. The Kshatriyas reinforced servility and deference to authority, while themselves being manipulated by the priests.

These cultural strata remain and intensify with geography. India is a place of great geographic diversity. The south, where few traders reached, remains the bastion of learning and produces the largest number of career (and IT) professionals. The west, with its thriving ports, is the hub of commerce. The north, known for its can-do attitude, was constantly invaded by outsiders. The northerners were forced to survive in the face of incessant onslaughts.

The east is an interesting confluence of commerce – it is the birthplace of the East India Company – and a bastion of intellectualism. Eastern India produced two Nobel laureates – Rabindranath Tagore and Amartya Sen. At the same time, the forward-thinking east embraced Marxism. And its flirtation with Marxism laid waste to the region's economy.

Just as the caste system helps develop an understanding of India, so does a quick political tour of the last century.

GANDHI AND NEHRU

Early in 1947, Mahatma Gandhi, (the Great Soul, Father of the Nation), met Lord Bevin, the personal emissary of British Prime Minister Winston Churchill, in Delhi. Bevin is reported to have told Gandhi, "Eighteen languages, 500 dialects, some 30 religions, a million Gods and Goddesses, 300 million individuals, an infinity of castes and sub castes, and a population (that is) practically illiterate and half of which (are) beggars or thieves . . . Good luck, sir! Such a nation is ungovernable! It'd take you centuries to get anywhere!"

Gandhi wrapped his large, white shawl a little more closely around him, and modestly replied, "India has eternity before her."

While India has a very long way to go, it has achieved much and overcome many of the obstacles in less than 60 years. I like to think that Lord Bevin and Winston Churchill would be surprised.

India's founding political leaders were divided philosophically. Mahatma Gandhi believed in private enterprise, but he was suspicious of technology and foreign investment. Jawaharlal Nehru, India's first prime minister, liked technology, but opposed private enterprise.

Gandhi was from the *Bania,* or merchant, class and related well with businessmen. He was from Gujarat, a land of seaports and vigorous commerce where merchants were held in relatively high esteem. He believed businessmen held their wealth in trust for society.

Nehru believed that the "commanding heights" of the economy – steel, power, and capital goods – were best controlled by government. Nehru was a Fabian socialist schooled in the elitist liberal ways. He was contemptuous of commerce. Nehru typified the "brown sahib" or "Englishmen without the English."

Gandhi, as immortalized in the Richard Attenborough movie that bears his name, returned to his roots in India at the age of 46 and became an evangelist for independence. He was the visionary, the chairman. Nehru was the chief executive leading India.

Unfortunately, the chairman's voice was silenced by an assassin only months after India gained its independence. Without Gandhi's leadership, India leaned toward socialism and geo-political tensions in the region.

It is important to note that the late Prime Minister Indira Gandhi, who was assassinated in 1984, is no relation to the elder Gandhi. She was the daughter of Nehru and married to a parliamentarian, Feroze Gandhi.

Since the early 1990s, the country has shaken off the Gandhi-Nehru legacy, for better and for worse. On the positive side, India has an active multi-party political system, economic reforms, and globalization. On the negative side, there has been sectarian violence and growing unrest with the economic status quo.

After breaking free from colonial rule, India emerged as one of the fastest developing economies in the world. It is the world's seventh largest country and second largest in population. India is also the largest democracy in the world. It's the world's second largest producer of rice, largest exporter of tea, jute, and of course, software. The country has developed its own supercomputer and is the second largest exporter of booster rockets for the space industry.

India has a parliamentary system of government with certain similarities to the U.S. system. There are two houses – a lower house known as Lok Sabha (House of People) and an upper house known as the Rajya Sabha (Council of States).

The Lok Sabha has 544 members, excluding the speaker, and the Rajya Sabha has 245 members. India has consistently maintained a healthy democracy since independence. The fact that India has not succumbed to dictatorships, military rule, or foreign invasion in the 50-plus years since independence is a testament to the basic strength of the country's government and institutions.

In the 1990s, India has been one of the fastest growing economies in the world. Indian average productivity levels double every 16 years. If the current pace of growth can be maintained, in 66 years India will have the same level of real GDP per capita as the U.S. today.

One of the main reasons foreign companies are eager to establish operations in India is to gain access to the growing middle class. By many measures it has 300 million today growing to 500 million by the end of the decade; a $2.9 trillion market growing to $9 trillion by 2020 on a PPP basis.

Indian Nobel Laureates

Literature 1913
TAGORE, RABINDRANATH,
b. 1861,   d. 1941

Physics 1930
RAMAN, Sir CHANDRASEKHARA VENKATA,
Calcutta University,
b. 1888,   d. 1970

Physiology or Medicine 1968 (1/3rd of prize)
KHORANA, HAR GOBIND,
U.S.A., University of Wisconsin, Madison, WI,
b. 1922 (in Raipur, India)

Physics 1983 (1/2 of prize)
CHANDRASEKHAR, SUBRAMANYAN,
U.S.A., University of Chicago, Chicago, IL,
b. 1910 (in Lahore, India),   d. 1995

Peace 1979
MOTHER TERESA,
leader of Missionaries of Charities, Calcutta,
b. 1910 (in Skoplje, then Turkey),   d. 1997

Economic Sciences 1998
SEN, AMARTYA,
Trinity College, Cambridge, Great Britain,
b. 1933

Graphic #20: Indian Nobel Laureates

Indian Role Models:

o The late American astronaut Kalpana Chawla first went into space aboard a NASA spacecraft in 1997. She died in the space shuttle disaster over Texas in 2003.

o Corporate leaders include Indira Nooyi, president and CFO of PepsiCo; Rajat Gupta, managing partner of McKinsey; and Victor Menezes, vice chairman of Citigroup.

o Entrepreneurs include Vinod Khosla, co-founder of Sun Microsystems; Sabeer Bhatia, founder of Hotmail; and Vinod Dham, father of the Pentium chip.

o Acclaimed laureates include Amartya Sen, winner of the Nobel Prize in Economics; and Subramanyan Chandrasekhar in Physics.

o Artists include Mira Nair, Monsoon Wedding; M. Night Shyamalan, The Sixth Sense and Signs; Salman Rushdie, author; and Vikram Seth.

> o   Political leaders (mostly outside the U.S.) from India in-
>   clude the Prime Minister of Mauritius, a Canadian cabinet
>   member, and several members of parliament in the U.K.
> o   Noted gurus include Mahesh Yogi and Deepak Chopra

TWO CULTURES: AMERICAN AND INDIAN

Some analysts believe that cultural differences between Indian IT vendors and their western customers will limit the ability of the Indian firms
to grow. Others believe that the cultural gulf between Indians and non-
Indians is not so great. I see signs that Indians are changing culturally on
almost a daily basis.

For example, the concept of taking responsibility for one's own career is new to the Indian workplace. In the past, Indian workers believed
that the company, not the individual worker, was primarily responsible
for their careers. Influenced by the American passion for taking charge of
one's own destiny, Indians are taking on responsibility for self-advance-
ment – seeking opportunities for additional training, new assignments,
and other career enhancers. It is a difficult adjustment that is happening
in years, not generations.

It is important for Indians to ensure that American, European, and
Japanese clients understand us and our cultural strengths and weaknesses.
Understanding is the key to developing an effective and profitable rela-
tionship.

The next several pages include brief summaries of some of the key
traits that are typically Indian.

DELIVERY OF BAD NEWS

No Indian likes to deliver bad news. In dealing with clients, Indians do
not like to be the bearer of bad news about a project, whether it concerns
the schedule or the workability of the project.

A British-born CIO with a U.K. client company told a story recently
that he announced at a project meeting with his Indian team that he

"would reward them if they told him he was wrong." All the Indian IT professionals sitting in the meeting nodded and smiled at the odd, but funny statement.

Yet not one offered him any bad news about the project or told him how something could be done better, despite the promise of a reward. The CIO had to repeat his statement several times before the Indian professionals began to understand what he was actually trying to say to them.

DEFERENCE TO AUTHORITY

Indian culture instills deference to authority. Indians do not like to disagree or contradict superiors, particularly in front of others. Typically, Indians will say what they think their superiors want to hear, not necessarily what is happening.

Indians will rarely look a superior in the eye. In India, eye contact is considered insolent. Most Indians, therefore, approach a superior with a bowed head.

TENDENCY TO OVER-PROMISE

Maybe it is our insecurities, but Indians tend to over promise. The desire to please is so ingrained, we commit to finishing a project on a schedule that is probably not feasible. But we commit to it anyway. It's called the "sure we can do that" syndrome. Then we put ourselves in the difficult position of having to tell the client it is not possible, or working very long hours to get it done – and making the project unprofitable for us.

DESIRE TO PRESERVE DIGNITY

This trait applies not only to one's self, but to others as well. The Indian culture does not encourage disagreements that may lead to the loss of dignity for anyone in the discussion. Thus, it is easy to build consensus on an idea or timetable among the Indians.

They will say "yes" when all they really mean is "yes, I have heard you." In this character trait, there are similarities to the Japanese and Chinese desire to save face and avoid confrontation.

USE OF BODY LANGUAGE OR INDIRECT COMMUNICATIONS

American business executives take pride in being blunt and straightforward in their speech. It is part of the John Wayne model of not "beating around the bush." But in many Asian cultures, including India, executives use indirect language and body language to express themselves. "I think so," in the U.S. means "probably." In India, it usually means "no."

If an Indian is asked in a meeting, "Is the project on schedule?" he might well respond: "Would you like it to be on schedule?"

Indians tend to stand closer to people they are conversing with when discussing a very important issue. They may shake their heads side to side to indicate "yes" – not "no" as in western culture. (The Indian side to side is usually swiveling the chin and top of head back and forth and not necessarily an American "no" twist of the head.) Indians tend not to respond when they disagree, which opens the door to misinterpretations.

GOOD AT TAKING DIRECTION

Indians are good at taking direction. This traces back to our system of education. We are less experienced at innovation.

School classrooms are organized differently in India than in the United States. Indian classrooms tend to be larger and more hierarchical. Students spend most of their time working on teacher-led activities as members of a whole class of students. Classes are much larger in India than in American schools. U.S. schools may average 24 students in the fifth grade, while the classrooms in Mumbai average 58.

These organizational differences translate into divergent patterns of thinking. American students spend much less time in school being attended to by the teachers, as compared to Indians. As a result, they are encouraged to have independent thought, as opposed to a collective thought.

INDIANS AND FOREIGNERS

Like everything else about it, India is both an open and a closed society. The long history of India and its interaction with invaders and conquerors shape and mold the way Indians work today with their foreign clients and foreign employers.

But India is changing. It is becoming a global society, and its people, culture, and industry are all influenced by its number one market – the U.S.

Nowhere has the change been more evident than in the emergence of the IT and IT-enabled industries. The rise of those industries will shape the Indian economy for years to come. The next chapter of this book looks at the Indian roots of these industries and how they evolved into today's economic drivers.

The passage to India is fascinating. Working with an Indian vendor presents some interesting challenges, first in selecting a vendor and then working closely with them to create the strategic advantages for which most corporations come to India.

The next section of this book also outlines how to pick a new Indian technology partner and suggests the best ways to work with that partner.

SECTION FIVE

GETTING IT DONE

"Execution is a specific set of behaviors and techniques that companies need to master in order to have a competitive advantage. It is a discipline of its own."
—Ram Charan, author and business advisor.*

Getting worried? Offshore options keeping you up at night?

Of course, it's perfectly natural for any CIO facing offshore outsourcing to have concerns about implementing a project in India. That's the very reason we wrote this book. Offshoring is interesting to read about, but it's another matter when it actually comes to taking action. As in any endeavor, there are right ways to do things . . . and wrong ways to do things.

In fact, there are probably many more ways to do something wrong than there are to do it right. I have years of experience with offshoring projects, and I would love to be able to tell you I never made a mistake, that all my projects went well. I'd love to be able to do that, but I can't. The good news is that, through this book, you can profit from what my colleagues and I have learned through hard experience.

---

*Execution: The Discipline of Getting Things Done, Publisher – Crown Business (June 2002)

This section of the book covers the basic requirements for conducting a successful project, starting with tips on how to choose a vendor with examples to illustrate how this can be done, and done well. Choosing a vendor takes some effort, but selecting the right partner is absolutely central to the success of any offshoring process.

WHAT PROJECTS SHOULD GO OFFSHORE?

As you can see from the accompanying illustration, there is a broad range of projects that make good candidates for offshore outsourcing. Obviously, the choice of the right project as the first to implement offshore is a crucial decision in the overall process. You can choose to follow either of two major philosophies:

1. The *Invisible Pilot Program* – Choose a small project, well out of view of senior management to minimize the risks overall.

2. The *Real Commitment Program* – Select a major program that requires serious senior management involvement and commitment.

It may seem counter-intuitive, but long experience shows that, without question, the *Real Commitment Program* is by far the better approach. It seems counter-intuitive because it looks like you're risking your life – at least your professional life – with a new organization.

Nevertheless, in this case intuition may be wrong. The natural instinct for professional self–preservation may, in fact, be destructive.

Services that can potentially leverage the offshore model include:

- Application Development
- Application Maintenance
- Enterprise Application Integration
- Package Implementation
- Platform Migration
- Legacy Transformation
- Global Roll-Outs Localization
- Testing & QA Services
- 24X7 Customer Support
- Help Desk Services

Graphic #21: What Can I Offshore?

First, implementing only a small project results in a scale of operation with only minimal cost savings, especially considering the business and technical talent the project will require. In many cases, such a project is too small for you and your staff to gain real insight into managing an offshore program.

Using the small project approach, you still have to do some significant "heavy lifting" when you move to a *Real Commitment* project. In addition, when senior corporate management suddenly "gets religion" – as they surely will when a fellow board member, an angry shareholder, or a golf buddy points out what competitors are doing (and how much money they're saving) – you risk considerable embarrassment . . . or worse.

On the other hand, implementing a larger, more significant program provides a real opportunity to show senior management what Indian offshoring can do for the company. Success in executing a major project can lead to a real partnership with your Indian vendor, which is the key to gaining the biggest payoff.

The larger the project, the more resources you can assign to it. And the larger the project, the more you can learn. Manage an offshore program of some scope, and you can leverage skills and knowledge better on future offshore projects. These skills can be used in subsequent projects with the same partner, or with other offshoring vendors.

On rare occasions, the CEO will "get religion" overnight – probably because of a sudden need to cut costs – and want to implement an offshoring program immediately. This may sound like a rare occurrence, but I've seen two examples of such a "Big Bang" approach. Count your blessings and hold on!

GETTING STARTED

The crucial step of deciding where you're going before setting out on your journey is often overlooked. After all, Columbus had no idea he found America. That's why we have the odd historical anomaly in which Native Americans were called "Indians."

The essential starting point for any offshoring experience is determining what the business needs and expects. Nothing is more important. The next step is to determine what you, as CIO, want to achieve. Is it strictly cost reduction? Are you trying to move the maintenance of legacy systems out of your organization? Do you want to upgrade the system architecture? Do you want to build a system that's beyond the skills available in-house?

These objectives must be clear and well understood by everyone involved. Then you can get the entire team's commitment. These objectives will play an important role in the selection process.

The next step – one of the most important – is selecting the vendor with whom you want to build this relationship. Finding a vendor is like matchmaking, and my native India, as you would expect, has a rich tradition of finding partners in diverse ways. In the Vedic times, suitors lined up and showed their athletic or military prowess to impress prospective brides and (more importantly) their families. In the worst chauvinistic period in recent times, prospective brides line up and show their parents' bank balances. In between these two extremes is a whole array of options ranging from the romantic to the astrological.

I can tell you from first hand experience that "soft" criteria, like feeling comfortable and trusting the vendor, are very important to the selection process. Unfortunately, they don't fit into a traditional selection matrix. They are hard to measure. Nevertheless, you must keep these criteria strongly in mind as the process proceeds.

First, decide how you want to make the selection. Methods range from looking to the East and hoping for a mystical vision to a highly structured Request for Information (RFI) / Request for Proposal (RFP) process. This structured process becomes even more rigorous, although somewhat removed, when consultants are brought in. The client, of course, is in the catbird seat because potential vendors – and there are a lot of them! – will break down your door.

Using an external consultant has real benefits. The consultant brings to bear a rigorous discipline on the selection and offshoring process. Vendors are judged on well-defined criteria, and rankings are captured for all relevant parameters. The process is typically carried out in a phased manner.

Vendors are taken through all the steps of evaluation and selection, from assessment to proposal evaluation, due diligence, contract development, and finally contract initialization. All client functions with a stake in the offshoring project — including human resources, finance, and general management — are involved at each step along with the IT department.

An independent, third party consultant helps establish the offshoring strategy and analyze the value created. The consultant assists in developing and designing the best solution, including negotiating the terms and conditions of the vendor contract. A consultant provides counsel on effective governance and change management procedures. All this ensures that you are as well prepared for your offshore journey as possible. Most importantly, a good consultant will ensure that you take the plunge.

Clearly consultants can carry you over the line smoothly, but staying with and gaining from the program is the client's responsibility.

COMPANY GENETICS

It is important to note that outsourcing vendors differ in some basic ways due to their origins. Their DNA evolved from different gene pools. Grouped by how they developed, the three basic types of Indian IT and BPO companies include:

- Staffing businesses
- Conglomerates that diversified into this business
- Entrepreneurial companies that specialize in delivering projects or products

As a result of their different origins, these companies have very different strengths and capabilities. For example, vendors that originated as staffing businesses are better at projects that involve personnel augmentation. They also tend to be better at the sales process because the staff augmentation business is a sales-intensive business.

Conglomerates have greater size and the ability to scale up quickly to handle large projects. Project/product companies deliver greater architectural skills and typically become strategic partners more readily.

Clients must keep these differences in mind during the selection process.

THE RFI / RFP PROCESS —
ASK THE RIGHT QUESTIONS

The following outline represents a selection process that should work well for most companies. First, on an informal basis narrow your list of potential vendors to no more than six. The informal basis should include a review of the company's origins and its reputation.

To the extent possible, compare prospective vendors to see if they match up well with your own needs at a high level. Determine whether you are looking for the largest and best known vendors, which have built their size and reputations on delivering quality work, or would prefer to work with mid-sized firms that might be more responsive to your needs.

PREPARE THE RFI

Preparing the RFI for these "short list" vendors is a critical step. The guidelines laid out in Appendix 1 should help considerably. The questions on the RFI should, of course, cover every area that is important to you. That said, it is important to resist the temptation to "torture" potential vendors by asking for too much detail at this point. But you can if you want to. It's your RFI.

Evaluate the RFI responses carefully. Meet with the vendors. Meet with their management teams and the key personnel that will work on the project. Evaluate each vendor's data centers and how they respond to requests and questions. This process will narrow the field dramatically.

Develop a comparison matrix and focus on the key criteria. Despite the scientific, computerized look to the results of such an analysis, they should not be the final word. After reviewing the results carefully, including your assessment of "soft" factors, select three finalists to go on to compete for the contract.

Keeping the field of candidates larger than this causes more work and effort on everyone's part – from your corporate management team to the vendors – to little purpose.

THE RFP PROCESS

The next step is the RFP process. Questions in the RFP are more detailed than the RFI and include a request for cost estimates. A sample list of RFP criteria is shown in Appendix 1. Some of the more subtle and often overlooked areas to examine include:

- What is the ratio of senior analysts and managers to junior programmers? (This ratio plays a key role in determining how quickly the vendor can ramp up, if that becomes necessary.)

· How much do they invest in R&D?

· What is their attrition rate? (This speaks to the kind of place it is to work in and the amount of time they spend in training.)

· With which technology companies are they partnered? (Be careful here; some vendors would partner with Daffy Duck. Be sure any partnerships are meaningful and that they have an in-depth knowledge of the vendor's technology or system.) What are the vendor's HR policies? (These are good indicators of how they will work with your people.)

· Does the vendor seem to be over-committing? (Sometimes it's better to have a vendor be candid about what they can't handle, rather than to find out the hard way they couldn't accommodate your needs after all.)

· Do all the vendors' references check out? (Include more than just those they supply. Contact top-level executives that are willing to discuss their relationship with the finalists.)

· Are the vendor's references long-time customers? (You must be able to gauge how well the vendor has responded to change and conflicts over the long term of the contract.)

At this phase of the process, ask each potential vendor to give a presentation to your staff and go through an interview process. You should speak directly with the senior management of prospective vendors. If at all possible, visit India and make on-site inspections. Be careful that you give each vendor the exact same time for presentation and access to you and your staff.

A Consultant's Role

An independent consultant could play a very helpful role in the selection process. Consultants can help manage the process and can provide benchmarking data which can be very helpful. The important caution here is that you be careful not to lose control of the process. At the end of the day, you will have to live with the result. The consultant will leave. The chart given on the next page summarizes the advantages and disadvantages of using a consultant.

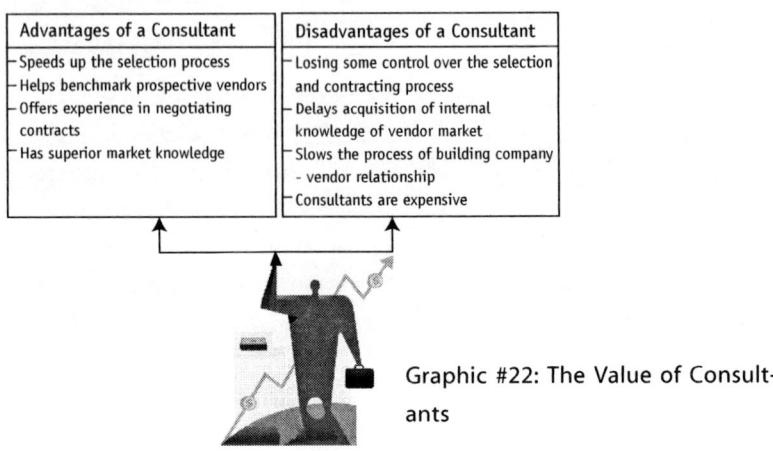

Advantages of a Consultant	Disadvantages of a Consultant

- Speeds up the selection process
- Helps benchmark prospective vendors
- Offers experience in negotiating
  contracts
- Has superior market knowledge
	- Losing some control over the selection
	  and contracting process
	- Delays acquisition of internal
	  knowledge of vendor market
	- Slows the process of building company
	  - vendor relationship
	- Consultants are expensive

Graphic #22: The Value of Consultants

RUNNING THE PROJECT

There is no shortage of project management books. I'm not about to write another. Rather, this book focuses on the unique aspects of managing an offshoring project. Consequently, I have not included the detailed process descriptions and documentation that are part of any well-managed project. Ultimately, the success of the project depends heavily on intangibles, such as building trust and the leadership's commitment to the success of the relationship.

Once the vendor is selected, the real fun starts. It's time to do the deal. In my experience, success in this aspect of the business is based on some high level alignment, including vision/goals, creating champion(s), transition and ongoing governance. But this is only the foundation. Sustained value comes through attention to detail, which is best *not* left to chance. It must be *processsized*.

The sections that follow will give you some ideas to incorporate into the process that you need to build. Remember this process should be built on the existing methodologies and cultures of your company.

Neglect any one of these factors and you'll end up in hot water. I can summarize all these factors in one word – *structure*. Everything you learned in

Management 101 applies here in spades. You are moving a key part of your company's operation thousands of miles away; a move like that requires serious attention to organization and process.

If you operate like some businesses do – "I gave that to Joe, he always gets it done." – rest assured that no matter how good Joe is, he can't pull this off on his own. If you let programmers operate independently, it's a habit you'll have to break. This is a team effort.

Football teams succeed by having pre-planned plays – blocking, running and passing as a team. This is an important caution to keep in mind while considering the various elements of managing a program – vision, governance, management, task definition and project planning, and project reporting. The process you build will include:

· Service Level Agreements (SLAs)
· Management Review
· Quality Assurance
· Change Management
· Risk Management
· Disaster Recovery
· Infrastructure

Many of these subjects are examined in detail below as we outline How to Run the Project.

THE "VISION THING"

Ensuring that the vendor's goals align with those of client management, the IT department, and with end users is critical. Getting quality code delivered on time and on budget may meet the contract specifications – but if the final product doesn't meet real business needs, then what?

For real program success the technical team must clearly understand the underlying business needs and goals of the end-user community, from the field sales force to staff functions, such as finance and human resources. Similarly, team members throughout the business must be fully aware of the technical development issues, challenges, and process.

Based on long experience, this vital step is best carried out through joint meetings among all parties, including executive sponsors, at least once every six months. This should include face-to-face meetings between the extended IT team and end users (business people).

GETTING TO KNOW EACH OTHER

Any successful off-shore relationship requires building real trust between two parties that are thousands of miles apart, come from different cultural backgrounds, and are literally in the dark when the other is in the light. To make the relationship work, the client corporation and the vendor must find common ground and build unwavering loyalty to one another.

This trust is built through investment of time and effort on both sides. Some practices and philosophies that help build that trust include making sure that:

- Client and vendor goals are fully aligned
- Leadership includes a "champion" for offshoring
- Expectations are carefully set
- All aspects of the project that will be most carefully reviewed (i.e., cost and schedule) have not been "over-promised"
- Schedules and deliverables are well defined

Having project champions in your organization is crucial to success. If senior management is fully committed to the project, it sets the tone for the entire team. Don't try to proceed without it. Senior management must understand the unique characteristics – and very real complexities – of offshoring, including a "feel" for Indian culture. Nothing beats a visit to India under your vendor's guidance.

Frankly, the failure of senior executives to visit India and meet their offshore partners in person signals a lack of corporate commitment. Invisible projects lead to invisible results. The champion needs to spearhead this commitment and get the entire project team excited about the project, as well.

TRANSITIONING – CRITICAL TO SUCCESS

The success of an offshore project often depends on making transitions . . . moving from the old, internal-only IT business model to one that embraces outsourcing. When done well – something that requires great attention to detail – transitioning builds confidence and trust . . . essential ingredients for success. On the other hand, if the needed transitions don't go smoothly, they may foreshadow additional problems later in the project. Like so many business endeavors, adequate planning for the transition is one of the keys to success.

Traditionally, Indian technology firms were weak in the important area of transitioning. Mastek/Majesco is investing considerable resources in this area that is critically important to the overall success of offshoring. Already, customers including ePolicy and the Lex Vehicle Leasing Company benefit from the company's enhanced focus on transitioning.

Depending on the scope of the project, client company teams involved in a variety of activities must plan and manage transition elements with various teams at the offshore partner. Examples might include the client company's customer support team working with the offshore maintenance team, or the maintenance team working with a U.S. onsite development team. Transitioning includes various types of hand-offs between the client and offshore teams. The hand-offs include problem tickets, impact analysis, estimates, test plans, test scripts, and status reports.

Activities involved in the transition to offshore outsourcing fall into four distinct phases:

- Study (planning)
- Onsite knowledge transition
- Offshore knowledge transition
- Steady state

The study, or planning, phase includes activities such as exercises between the two teams in vision alignment; setting expectations regarding SLA terms and conditions, processes, standards and guidelines, and quality indicators.

Onsite knowledge transition involves training for the vendor Project Managers and should be conducted onsite in the U.S. This training covers both technical and business issues and includes subject matter such as specific tools, functional area/domain knowledge, testing and quality management, release management, build management, configuration management, operations, and more. After the completion of training activities, the vendor team should "shadow" key client team operations. Shadowing exercises ultimately graduate to a reversal of roles, with vendor team members performing the work while client personnel review the work products.

Offshore knowledge transition activities should be simultaneous with the onsite deployment of vendor personnel at the client facilities. In this phase, key members of the U.S.-based development team are introduced to the offshore facility to establish and test the development environment. Key components include establishing communication links including e-mail, video conferencing, and a common workflow-based knowledge repository; setting up the development environment; and enabling other key areas of the needed infrastructure.

SLA terms and conditions should be identical for onsite and offshore teams. During this period, two functional vendor teams exist – an onsite and an offsite team, and the high-priority/complexity problems are routed through the onsite team. As the offshore team gains demonstrated competency, an increased number of Priority Level 1 and Level 2 problems will be moved offshore. The client should then conduct an evaluation of the offshore team's performance and deliverable quality. Once that is completed, the vendor can begin to transition its onsite team to the offshore facility.

One aspect of Mastek/Majesco investment in transitioning is a project training management database to maintain a thorough skills inventory for each consultant, monitor expected roll-off dates, and manage training forecasts and demand. This database allows us to identify and plan the deployment of highly qualified resources for scheduled assignments or provide short-term assistance with challenging issues or unexpected ramp-ups. This approach is one way we help achieve the final phase of transitioning – the "steady state" required for smooth ongoing project execution.

GOVERNANCE — THE OVERLOOKED PROCESS

	CUSTOMER	OFFSHORE COMPANY	
Executive Board	CIO BUSINESS SPONSOR	PRESIDENT V.P. - BUSINESS UNIT	Strategic Planning Executive Preview Dispute Resolution
Governance Office	PROGRAM MANAGER BUSINESS MANAGER	ACCOUNT MANAGER	Tactical Planning Performance Evaluation Issue Resolution Approvals Financial Management Contract Amendment Relationship Management
Project Management	SUPPORT MANAGER	PROJECT MANAGER	Policy & Procedure Definition Release Planning Change Management Delivery Management Issue Resolution Continuous Improvement

Graphic #23: Typical Governance Model

Governance is not the same as management. In most cases, the CIO and his/her team are the project "owners" and managers. The corporate Board of Directors is responsible for governance. Recent events demonstrate clearly the importance of the governance function. Governance is every bit as formal a process as management, and you should treat it as such.

The governance process is the means by which the program is managed and reviewed at the senior level. The structure above shows a series of parallel levels between the offshore vendor's organization and the client organization. It's important to understand how these levels operate.

CIO / VENDOR PRESIDENT

There must be open communications between the client CIO and the head of the vendor organization. These leaders need to agree on the vision, pace, teaming strategies, and review mechanisms. Offshoring is gut wrenching at times, and the heads of the two organizations must be aligned to prevent cracks from forming and to help navigate the inevitable tight corners, such as scope creep, budget squeeze, and critical person dependencies.

This cooperation works both formally and informally. The formal part of the project consists of regularly scheduled reviews, no more than one month apart. These reviews enable frequent updates, technical problem resolution, solving staffing problems, and other matters that cannot be resolved at lower management levels. Experience teaches that these regular meetings should be scheduled well in advance and that both executives make a firm commitment to attend every meeting, without exception.

The informal approach builds trust among the top management team. They are in a fish bowl and their behavior determines the larger organizational interaction. A client recently asked me and our team to join a surprise Indian Independence Day party (August 15th) that the COO of the client organization had initiated! We were impressed – first that he even knew when Indian Independence Day is celebrated – and secondly that he would seize the opportunity to build an informal relationship.

BUSINESS SPONSOR /
VENDOR VP

The head of the business unit sponsoring the project will work with the vendor vice president responsible for this program. Here too, a close bond between these key executives has a big impact on the project. It is their mutual role, of course, to ensure that the project is meeting the business objectives set out for the program. They need to translate the business goals into technology deliverables and make the inevitable trade offs. In addition, these managers need to recognize that people are more comfortable when the software is developed next door . . . and that writing code from afar impacts the richness of communication.

The business unit head should be a part of the project team, monitoring the project to ensure it is clearly meeting his business needs. You need strong commitment from this individual – do everything you can to get it since this will prove critical when the going gets rough.

The experience of a mid-sized insurance company on the East Coast is instructive. We had strong, transparent relationships with key stake-holders across the client organization. The project started as a fairly straightforward legacy migration. Midstream, however, the solution had to be redone due to some newly introduced government statutes for that particular industry.

These changes took time to implement, and schedules were pushed out considerably. The business unit head did not, however, ask for our heads on a platter. We took great pains to keep him informed at all stages of the development process. He knew the reasons behind the delays and supported us in extending and meeting the new deadline.

EXECUTIVE BOARD

The four executives defined in the section above constitute the project's Executive Board. They serve as the Board of Directors, constantly reviewing progress and direction. They meet regularly, very likely on a monthly basis, and constantly reassess strategy, review top-level status, resolve disputes, and take whatever management action may be necessary. Once again, formal processes are essential to the success of the board . . . and the overall project.

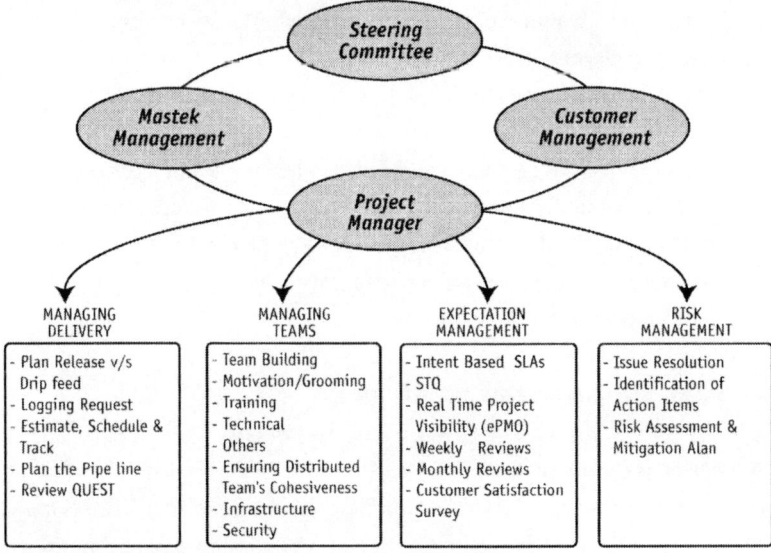

Graphic #24: Majesco's Engagement Model

BUSINESS MANAGER / PROGRAM MANAGER / VENDOR ACCOUNT MANAGER

The business manager of the sponsoring business unit, your IT group's program manager, and the vendor's account manager constitute the Governance Office. These executives are responsible for issues like financial performance,

129

contractual issues, and overall administration of the relationship. This is the classic purchasing officer versus account manager face-off. It is extremely important, but must not be bureaucratic or adversarial. As in the example of corporate governance, this group obviously plays a key role in ensuring the success of the program.

The case of the East Coast insurance company again comes to mind. The delays in getting the project completed added unplanned costs. There were two key people from the client's organization who had the expertise to adapt the company's insurance instruments to the government's new statutes. The project could proceed only after the instruments were modified.

As it happened, both these men were on vacation. Nothing much was done until their return. There was quite a bit of confusion about how these costs would get shared. We had billed the client for the time that our people were forced to sit waiting for the necessary input. The client wanted to go by the fixed price terms of the contract agreement. It easily could have developed into a classic confrontation.

But no. Nothing of the sort happened. Our people sat down with their people and reviewed the sequence of events leading to the cost overrun in detail. The client understood and accepted our reasons for additional charges and paid the invoice. This amicable resolution was possible largely, and maybe only, because of the excellent relationship that the client's manager shared with Mastek/Majesco's account manager.

PROJECT MANAGEMENT OFFICE

A key step is the appointment of a Support Manager responsible for managing any client resources provided for the offshoring program. The Support Manager works with the vendor's Project Manager on day-to-day project management issues. These include release planning, change management, issue resolution, the continuous improvement process, and more.

RIGHT METHODOLOGY —
THE METHOD BEHIND THE PROCESS

An important part of offshoring development work is choosing the right project lifecycle methodology. There are several methodologies, and you should take care to use the one best suited to you, your organizational strengths, and development risks.

Remember at all times that project lifecycle models are not interchangeable. To deliver a quality system, it's critical to know the risks facing the project and to use a model that reduces those risks. It is important that we review some standard project lifecycle models – and their strengths and weaknesses. What model do you use? Or, more appropriately, what model should you use? The following summary should help you decide.

Pure Waterfall

This is the classical system development model. It consists of the following discontinuous phases:

- Concept
- Requirements
- Architectural design
- Detailed design
- Coding and development
- Testing and implementation

> *Strengths:* This model minimizes planning overhead since it can be done upfront; the structure minimizes wasted effort, so it works well for technically weak or inexperienced staff.

> *Weaknesses:* Lack of flexibility; only the final phase produces a non-documentation deliverable; backing up to address mistakes is difficult

> *Summary:* The pure waterfall performs well for products with clearly understood requirements, or when working with well understood technical tools, architectures, and infrastructures. Its weaknesses frequently make it inadvisable when rapid development is needed. In those cases, modified models may be more effective.

Spiral

The spiral is a risk-reduction oriented model that breaks a software project up into mini-projects, each addressing one or more major risks. After major risks have been addressed, the spiral model terminates as a waterfall model. Spiral iterations involve the following six steps:

- Determine objectives, alternatives, and constraints
- Identify and resolve risks
- Evaluate alternatives
- Develop the deliverables for that iteration and verify that they are correct
- Plan the next iteration
- Commit to an approach for the next iteration

Strengths: Early iterations of the project are the cheapest, enabling the highest risks to be addressed at the lowest total cost. This ensures that as costs increase, risks decrease; each iteration of the spiral can be tailored to suit the needs of the project.

Weaknesses: It is complicated and requires attentive and knowledgeable management to pull it off.

Summary: For projects with risky elements, it's beneficial to run a series of risk-reduction iterations which can be followed by a waterfall or other non-risk-based lifecycle.

Modified Waterfall

The modified waterfall uses the same phases as the pure waterfall, but is not done on a discontinuous basis. This enables the phases to overlap when needed. The pure waterfall can also split into subprojects at an appropriate phase (such as after the architectural design or detailed design).

Strengths: More flexibility than the pure waterfall model;

if there is personnel continuity between the phases, documentation can be substantially reduced; implementation of easy areas do not need to wait for the hard ones

Weaknesses: Milestones are more ambiguous than for the pure waterfall; activities performed in parallel are subject to miscommunication and mistaken assumptions; unforeseen interdependencies can create problems

Summary: Risk reduction spirals can be added to the top of the waterfall to reduce risks prior to the waterfall phases. The waterfall can be further modified using options such as prototyping or other methods of requirements gathering done in overlapping phases.

RATIONAL UNIFIED PROCESS OR RUP

The Rational Unified Process or RUP is a productized process developed by Rational Software. RUP provides an iterative approach to software development dividing each project into several small projects that run sequentially, one after another. Each iteration has a well defined set of objectives, and concludes by delivering an executable that is a step closer to the final product than the last one. Each iteration contains elements of requirement management, analysis and design, implementation, and testing. The process divides a software project into four phases: Inception, Elaboration, Construction and Transition.

Inception: Understand what to build
Elaboration: Understand how to build it
Construction: Build a beta version of the product
Transition: Build the final version of the product

Strengths: Iterative approach allows for an increasing understanding of the problem through successive refinements and incrementally grows an effective solution over multiple iterations. Customers see steady progress; this is useful when requirements are changing rapidly, when the customer is reluctant to commit to a set of requirements, or when no one fully understands the application area.

Weaknesses: It is impossible to know at the outset of the project how long it will take; there is no way to know the number of iterations that will be required. The RUP approach requires a lot of investment in tools for effectiveness.

Summary: The manager must be vigilant and ensure this approach doesn't become an excuse to revert to code-and-fix development.

These standard models can be adapted to fit the industry issues, corporate culture, time constraints, and team vulnerabilities which comprise your environment. Discuss these in detail with your offshore partner to come up with the methodology to match your needs. Integrating methodologies is an on-going responsibility ranging from adopting a common approach to ensuring compatibility of tools.

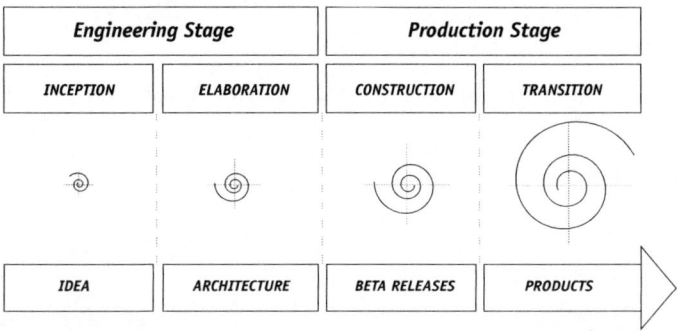

Engineering Stage		Production Stage	
INCEPTION	ELABORATION	CONSTRUCTION	TRANSITION
IDEA	ARCHITECTURE	BETA RELEASES	PRODUCTS

PHASES

Disciplines	Inception	Elaboration	Construction	Transition
Business Modelling				
Requirements				
Analysis & Design				
Implementation Test				
Deployment				
Configuration & Change Mgmt.				
Project Management				
Environment				
	Initial	Elab#1 Elab#2	Const#1 Const#2 Const#2	Tran#1 Tran#2

ITERATIONS

Graphic #25: Spiral and RUP Methodologies

MANAGING ALL THE MOVING PARTS

It is important to remember that *Program Management* and *Program Governance* are different. To put it in slightly different terms, management takes place below deck where the team makes sure the engine is running; governance takes place on the Captain's bridge.

At the risk of appearing redundant, the simple fact is that, here again, *process is the key*. Rather than presenting a "Management 101" discussion of management structure, let's turn to a review of some unique aspects of managing an offshore program. Stop for a minute and consider again what you are trying to do – move a significant part of your company's IT function to a location thousands of miles away. You have to respect the magnitude of such a project.

The infrastructure underlying the program – both hardware and software – must be managed both at your location and the vendor's location. It must support all development work being done at both locations, as well as the transfer of software and data between locations. Obviously, the infrastructure must operate 24x7 with very high availability.

The importance of this aspect to the success of the overall project means there must be an *Infrastructure Manager* on the team reporting to the Program Manager. While infrastructure is crucial on any project, it is particularly challenging when two sites thousands of miles apart have a completely interconnected infrastructure.

There are basically two options when it comes to putting your infrastructure in place, as follows:

Option 1: *Have Identical Development Environments in Both Places*

The benefit of replicating environments is that work at each site is independent of the other, and each side can proceed according to their own pace. The drawback is that it's hard to merge the results into common source code. In addition, since the method calls for two complete development sites, this approach is relatively expensive.

Option 2: *Work Remotely On the Client Site from the Offshore Location*

By having the offshore site appear as additional terminals to the onshore site, setup costs are minimized and the configuration is easy to manage. On the other hand, this method is critically dependent on the stability and availability of the telecommunication connection.

There are numerous variations of these two models, which depend on the manner in which the software is to be managed and tested for inclusion in the baseline code set. We will not go into these variations, but conclude this topic by emphasizing the importance of planning the onsite/offshore combined environment carefully.

Quality Assurance and Testing plays an important role in an offshoring program. A *QA and Testing Manager* is another team member reporting to the Program Manager. The *QA and Testing Manager* performs the usual roles with which you are familiar. Error rates must be carefully measured when used to monitor program quality, and feedback systems should be put in place to track and focus on the sources of errors. Finally, the program plan may call for 24 hour-a-day testing by having the testing "follow the sun" around the globe between the U.S. and India. This can be a major factor in reducing the project schedule.

You will need a manager responsible for your team; the vendor will likewise need a manager for its team, both on-site and offshore.

GETTING THE PLAN TOGETHER

The Program Manager and his management team lay out a task breakdown. They use the management structure to solicit planning data. For each task they must define the following:

- The objective and deliverables of the task
- The person responsible for the completion of each task
- Reporting requirements
- The type of resources required
- The length of time each resource is needed
- The inter-dependencies between the tasks

THE INTERNET FOR REPORTING —
STAY ONLINE TO STAY ON TRACK

Information from each of these areas is entered into a project management software tool. This tool allows the Program Manager to see conflicts and problem areas. The program also provides a very accurate estimate of the manpower demand over time.

As the project proceeds, task completion data is entered into the program to re-estimate cost and projects the date by which all areas involved will be moved offshore. The management team uses these results to take the appropriate action.

Accurate and timely project reporting allows managers to make changes and take corrective action quickly, when it can be most effective. That is a challenge. Mastek/Majesco developed a system that allows everyone involved in the off-shore project to track progress at various levels – from a general overview of how the project is going to data on whether an individual programmer is on target.

The system is called e-PMO for e-Project Management Office. It is a powerful project monitoring and control solution. Web-enabled, e-PMO provides the entire management team access to project status information from anywhere on the globe. The information on project status and project metrics is shown in a graphic format.

Each project is tracked along five principles of Quality, Utilization, Efficiency, Scope, and Timeliness (QUEST). The review chart is a graphic tool that reviews project status in real time. The tool provides drill-down capabilities to analyze the information from the overall project level down to the lowest activity level.

MASTEK EPMO

Graphic #26: ePMO: The Control Panel – Online interactive management dashboard that monitors project status and customizes service delivery in real time

Managers at all levels on both the customer and vendor teams use the e-PMO system to know exactly where the project stands at any moment, resource utilization and burn rates, and whether the vendor is meeting the milestones. Data is acquired on a minute-by-minute basis – some by automated tools, some by manual entry.

PUT SERVICE LEVEL AGREEMENTS IN PLACE

Mastek/Majesco always prepares a formal SLA so everyone is clear on what is to be delivered, and when. The SLA should spell out items such as:

- The description of the deliverable, which may include a service, such as set up of a customer service center
- The date of delivery
- Responsibility for delivery
- Responsibility for acceptance
- Acceptance criteria
- If appropriate, quantitative quality requirements

Everyone involved with the particular service or delivery signs off on the SLA. No changes are permitted without a formal request, SLA revision, and sign-off on the new SLA. This is a lot of process, as usual, but it goes a long way in preventing misunderstanding.

Another technique that is very useful is something known as a "RACI" matrix to spell out and clarify team responsibilities.

	Description	No. allowed per task
Responsible	**"The Doers"** Execute the task and create the deliverable(s); involve others as needed	Many
Accountable	**"The Owner"** Ensures the task is completed and appropriate procedures, tools, and templates are used	One
Consulted	**"The Experts"** Are involved during the task and contribute to the deliverable(s) as requested, or as they deem appropriate	Many
Informed	**"The Stakeholders"** Are provided with the final deliverable after it is complete, but do not contribute to it	Many

Graphic #27: RACI Overview – The RACI framework defines how different roles work together to complete tasks and deliverables

The matrix acronym RACI comes from the fact that the matrix divides roles into the following categories;

R — *Responsible*
A — *Accountable*
C — *Consulted*
I — *Keep Informed*

An example of a RACI matrix is shown below.

	Training Development	Beta Test Plan	Customer Acceptance Readiness Review	Beta Testing	Production Environment Set-up/Upgrade	Training Plan Implementation	Customer Support Plan Implementation	Marketing Communication Plan Implementation	Deployment Readiness Review
Client									
Program Manager (PMO)			AR						AR
Release Team Leader		C	R	I	A	I	I	I	R
Business System Analysts	R		C	I		R	I	I	C
Quality Assurance		AR	C	A					C
Product & Marketing Management	I	C	C	I		I	I	AR	C
Customer Service & Support	AR	C	C	I		AR	AR	I	C
ITS			C		R				C
End-user Pilot Group		C		R					
Majesco									
Account Manager			I						I
Program Manager (PMO)			AR						AR
Project Team Leader			C	I					C
System Analysts			I	I					I
Solution Architect			I	I	I				I
Integration/Portal Lead			I						I
Developers									
Quality Assurance									
Configuration Manager									
Vendor									
Account Manager	C								
System Analysts	C								
Product Architect	C								
Technical Staff									

Graphic #28: RACI Sample — Majesco's RACI Chart for the Release Lifecycle of a Project

DON'T GET CAUGHT

Audits are necessary to ensure process compliance. The primary objective is to ensure that the project team is adhering to the software development practices and project management standards in the areas of Requirement Management, Scheduling, Tracking, Monitoring, Configuration Management, Quality Management, and Risk Management throughout the project life cycle.

QA is important in any project, but there are some QA aspects that are particularly important in offshoring. First, the standard requirement that all testing results be documented is now **absolutely essential**. There is no way the onshore and offshore team can manage the error resolution feedback process without absolute adherence to precise documentation.

Second, an important part of the QA loop is input from the business executives, many of whom are not used to this level of control. You must get their input into the process – their input is probably the most important.

A unique aspect of an offshoring program is the potential for testing 24x7 by moving testing to India at night. This factor is successful on many projects producing significant schedule improvements. Success with this approach requires careful planning involving procedures, infrastructure, and documentation.

It's likely that your vendor partner has a CMM-5 shop, which includes extensive QA testing implications. While you will not, and should not, turn your organization into a CMM-5 shop, there are procedures to be learned and adopted. An important example is the process for dealing with errors found by QA testing. The team will, of course, correct each error. Perhaps more importantly, in a CMM-5 organization the source of the error is found and fixed. This has important implications, and should be baked into the project QA process.

How Do I Change My Mind?

The easiest and most foolproof way to lose control of your project is failure to control the change request process. Each change request must be documented. The documentation should include:

- The person requesting the change
- A clear description of the change
- The reason for the change
- Priority level
- Schedule requirements

When a Change Request is received, it should be logged and dated. The request is then sent to the organization responsible for the change to get an estimate of resource requirements and schedule impact. This information is documented and attached to the Change Request. The request then goes to the Program Manager who works with the team to determine how best to deal with the request. The action decided on is documented and sent to both the manager responsible for making the change and to the person requesting the change.

This procedure should be followed for every Change Request, regardless of where it originates.

WHAT CAN GO WRONG?

Murphy said it best: If it can go wrong, it will. That's why the best execution plans include extensive preparation for errors, mistakes, and outright disasters.

Most Indian firms focus heavily on risk management, identifying and planning for a wide variety of potential risks that may threaten a project execution. Some of the most obvious risks are:

- Human factors
- Processes (or the absence of processes) at the client or development site
- Technology issues – hardware or software
- Hardware environment
- Software environment
- Unpredictable integration issues with external systems
- Unforeseen business requirements

Many risks can be minimized by following quality procedures and monitoring. Risk prevention is built into quality procedures from the contract development through implementation.

Every identified risk in a project should be classified. For the most serious threats, managers should conduct a regular review to ensure that they can spot the threats and take remedial action against them before they become more serious threats.

Develop a formal Risk Management Plan (RMP) to identify potential risks and devise a plan for dealing with each risk. The RMP creates the framework for risk identification, risk mitigation, and the ability to raise early warnings when risks are detected. It also provides a mechanism for consistent evaluation of risks throughout the project life cycle.

One project for a Fortune 500 financial services firm illustrates the dangers of improper risk management. The project got off track quickly because client management, lacking experience in offshoring, failed to devote sufficient time and attention to defining the project. At the same time, as a vendor working with a new client, we failed to invest enough time and effort to educate the client about offshoring and the amount of time and effort it would require – at least in the beginning.

The specific issue was that neither the client nor the vendor exerted the discipline needed to define the project correctly or to manage the inevitable scope creep.

As the work started, additional requirements kept cropping up. Despite assigning more people than budgeted, the project was completed months behind schedule as a result of scope creep. Because this was a fixed-price contract, our company lost money on the additional resources. More importantly, the client lost opportunities to sell the product to a large number of waiting customers. The delay caused the client to be late in meeting its time-to-market commitments. Both sides suffered in a classic Lose-Lose scenario.

Another major problem was that project management on the client side was assigned to an inexperienced and junior executive. At the same time, the project manager on the vendor side exhibited some characteristics that are very typically Indian (see Section 4 for a list of those traits).

As the project got off-track, the inexperienced manager consulted with the eager to please Indian manager on solutions, but nothing was documented. The Indian manager constantly agreed to provide additional work and reassured the client manager that all would be accomplished. This mutual back scratching succeeded in keeping the early signs of trouble under management's radar. When things finally spiraled out of control, it was unfortunately too late to fix.

You must ensure that this does not happen to you. Do not throw the project over the wall and wait for it to come back on time and in perfect shape. It won't happen. To paraphrase a popular saying, "Stuff happens." With proper risk management, it won't.

There are many lessons learned on both sides of a client/vendor relationship. Some clients believe they know how to outsource work offshore, only to find well into the project that they don't know everything. Similarly, the vendor must learn to work with each new client, adapting their processes – and even their culture – to match those of the client.

With one large software company, my company stubbed its entire foot on a project. The client company typically bought off-the-shelf products, adapted them, and then tested them before putting going to market. It had never before worked with a subcontractor that built the product from the ground up. As a result, the client software company greatly underestimated the amount of time it would take to test and approve work sent from India.

The company thought offshoring was like a black box – feed specifications in one end and great products come out the other end. Based on this belief, the company chose not to have an on-site coordinator, increasing the communications and coordination work load for both companies.

The project got off-track and tempers began to flare to the point that more time was spent fighting among the teams, rather than working on the project. At that point – just short of the company canceling the project – two managers, the vice president for architecture on the client side and the project manager on the Mastek side, stepped in. They had a good working relationship and trusted one another. They issued an edict to the staff that declared the combatants had at most 48 hours to resolve any problem at the staff level. If they could not resolve the issue in that time, it was to be escalated to the managers, who together made a ruling. That process, built on a good working relationship between two managers, saved the project and helped deliver a quality product.

IF DISASTER STRIKES

Since the attacks of 9/11, the possibility of terrorist attacks and war are far greater concerns for many corporations. When India and Pakistan reached the brink of war – including the possible use of nuclear weapons – availability of backup facilities and continuity of service were major concerns.

Disasters are a fact of life. They are not limited to offshore companies.

What if another earthquake hits northern California? What about terrorist attacks?

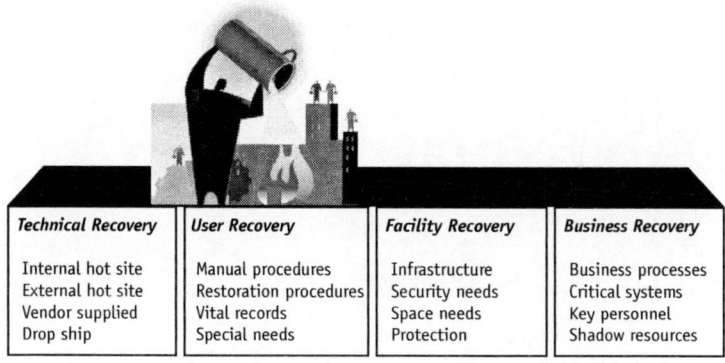

Technical Recovery	User Recovery	Facility Recovery	Business Recovery
Internal hot site	Manual procedures	Infrastructure	Business processes
External hot site	Restoration procedures	Security needs	Critical systems
Vendor supplied	Vital records	Space needs	Key personnel
Drop ship	Special needs	Protection	Shadow resources

Graphic #29: Disaster Recovery Strategies

Some progressive offshore companies, like Mastek/Majesco, maintain backup centers in other countries in case of political turmoil or major natural disasters. Surprisingly, many American companies don't insist on a Disaster Recovery Plan from their vendor.

Any offshoring program must include creation of a Continuity of Business (COB) plan. The team is responsible for all responses during and after any disaster, and for managing the business continuity process.

Many firms maintain a well-crafted COB plan. For example, we have a Service Continuity site at Pune, India because that city is in a different seismic zone from Mumbai. Should an earthquake hit Mumbai, Pune is almost 200 miles away. We maintain additional resources and space in Kuala Lumpur, Malaysia. This facility can accommodate additional people in the event we ever need to transfer development and maintenance functions outside India. In addition, we have facilities in Bristol, England – a geo-politically stable area – as additional back-up in the event of a disaster in India. Both the Pune and Bristol facilities are networked with our development centers in Mumbai and Mahape and can meet the requirements for our COB plan.

We are prepared to move project teams from Mumbai to Pune on four hours' notice. Similarly, we can move teams to the U.K. within 24 hours.

Graphic #30: Emergency Back up Sites

THE PLUMBING

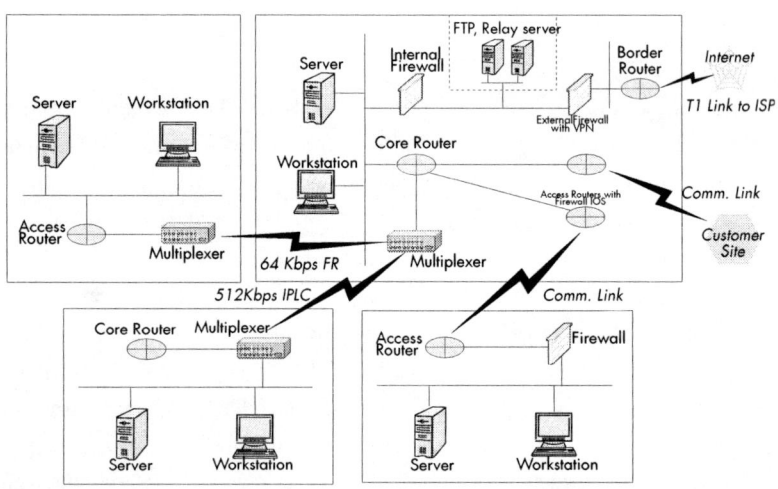

Graphic #31: The Plumbing – Worldwide networking infrastructure that makes it all happen. The figure above shows the infrastructure of a typical offshoring project – sometimes referred to as "the plumbing." It shows high-speed lines between your site and the vendor's site in India. Provision must be made for backup so that no project time is lost due to an outage.

A team including infrastructure experts from your organization and the vendor's organization is responsible for designing and maintaining the structure. The design of an effective, highly available network and development environment is a crucial success factor.

The development and testing environment at the vendor's site must be a close replica of the in-house corporate site in both hardware and software. A single set of software at both sites manages the development process, staff utilization, error rate (a surrogate for quality), and progress to date measured on a *daily* basis.

As described earlier, infrastructure requires a manager, reporting to the Program Manager, since a significant part of the initial design effort must be devoted to designing the program infrastructure.

Now we are ready to get started; take that first step toward offshoring. It is a very exciting time to make this venture. Whether you work for a Fortune 1000 company or a mid-sized company, offshoring will change the way you have done many things in the past. It will create new opportunities and new challenges – both helping you and your company to grow.

There is more to learn about the processes and much more to think through – particularly the relationship you will have with your partner in India. Remember, the more you make your partner a part of your company, the better results you can expect.

APPENDIX 1 – VENDOR SELECTION CRITERIA

THE RFP

Ideally, an RFP asks all pertinent questions about the methodologies, technology, and experience of a potential vendor. The vendor's responses should supply answers to these questions and hopefully impart additional information and insights about its capabilities. A good RFP must be well designed to elicit competitive responses. This is critical for effective evaluation and comparison of multiple vendors' abilities.

The typical offshoring RFP broadly covers the following:

1. Executive Summary
2. Vendor Profile
3. Business Condition
4. Corporate Practices and Procedures
5. Use of Benchmarking
6. Proposed Services
7. Overall Approach
8. Engagement Models
9. Conformance to Client Requirements
10. Application Development Services
11. Offshoring Methodology

12. Project Management Plan
13. Resource Plan
14. Expandability and Change Management
15. Infrastructure Capabilities
16. Risks and Contingency Plan
17. Technical and Business Solution
18. Service Levels and Penalties
19. Processes to Monitor Progress and Measure Results
20. Escalation Procedures and Issue Resolution
21. Customer Base
22. Business Profile and Strategy
23. Termination and Exit Options/Strategies
24. Appendices and Case Studies
25. References

Each RFP is issued, of course, for a particular project or set of projects. Consequently, the RFP should capture any details that are particular to the project(s) under consideration. Questions about the project scope, expected results, commercial terms and conditions, security/data protection, and other such information will by necessity vary from RFP to RFP. As a representative illustration, however, the following excerpt from a sample RFP shows the kind of specific information you should set out to gather.

SAMPLE OFFSHORE OUTSOURCING RFP

Features and Functionality

1. On what framework do you propose to build our company's application, keeping in mind primary factors such as: scalability, "statefulness", interface capability, and the business and functional requirements of the application?

2. Describe how the application you build will provide business rules. Clarify whether the product will be component-based or run as a separate service.

3. Describe your methodology's rule building environment and how it works. Address specific visual or natural language interfaces available for the rule building process. Describe any rule debugging facilities, as well as any extensions like rule versioning, you feel are important.

4. How will your application monitor and minimize system performance impact? Describe any architectural features or controls that minimize performance impact upon the application employing the rules engine.

5. How are updated rules made available to the engine or applications relying on them? Are rule changes available to the application component on a real time basis?

6. What product services are available to support our ongoing development efforts? For example, what features support our use of the product through a development environment, into an integration testing environment, and finally into a quality assurance environment?

7. Describe your methodology's support for J2EE, XML, BEA's Web Logic, Sun's Solaris, Oracle, and Netegrity's Siteminder. Include product versions where applicable.

Security

1. Describe how your application will include the ability to encrypt data in transmission, memory, or storage. If it cannot encrypt data, what encryption hardware or software can it be integrated with? Our company's accepted encryption methodologies are as follows:

    a. Symmetric: DES or 3DES3, Message Authentication Code (MAC)
    b. Asymmetric: Digital Signature Standard using the Secure Hash Algorithm (SHA-1), RSA

2. Detail how you will construct the system's audit log captures for security purposes, if not already detailed in section above. For example, will the system log all password changes, successful and unsuccessful logon attempts, changes to privileges and access rules, etc.?

3. How will you provide an audit log that is tamper proof and provides non-repudiation?

Pricing

1. Please provide a pricing proposal for completion of this project – including all costs you anticipate will be incurred to develop this application – and be sure to address:

    a. Project management time/cost
    b. Development time/cost
    c. Software licensing
    d. Equipment purchases
    e. Travel costs as appropriate

2. Describe your typical pricing structure (e.g., hourly, flat fee per proposal, etc.).

3. How would you configure a pricing proposal for our solution?

4. Describe the pricing structure of product upgrades or enhancements if requested.

5. What are the scoping and set-up costs? How do you scope a project, and how long does it usually take? How often has your initial scope reconciled with the end result?

6. Describe the type of professional services you offer in conjunction with development.

7. Do you see any additional hardware costs for the requirements we have outlined? If so, what equipment would you propose and what is the estimated cost of that equipment?

8. Does your company also provide ongoing maintenance? What are the annual maintenance costs? What is covered by maintenance?

Volumes/Scalability

1. Our application currently averages 50 concurrent users. We would like to expand capacity to handle 400 concurrent users. What changes, if any, would you propose to architecture, hardware, infrastructure, etc. to handle this volume?

2. Comment on the scalability of the framework you would use overall.

3. Can you provide scalability and performance benchmarks?

4. Does your organization provide ongoing post-production support of the applications you develop?

5. Provide a timeline/project plan for scoping, gathering requirements, and developing the application. In particular, comment on the elapsed number of months you anticipate this project will take to complete, as well as what you consider major contingencies in meeting the proposed timeline.

6. If you answered yes to question 4 above, please describe pricing for ongoing support and maintenance (e.g., pricing per call, per month, by annual contract, etc.).

7. Do you provide 24x7x365 support? Is this support included in basic pricing?

8. What service level agreement do you guarantee to customers that

use your support?

Other Information/Requests

1. We will provide 1 FTE resource to work with your organization to complete this project. How would you propose to use this resource? The objective would be to use this resource as a link providing knowledge transfer both from the existing application to development of the new application and as subsequent knowledge transfer from the new application back to our development and business groups.

2. Describe your development strategy over the past several years, i.e., how did your organization become what it is today?

3. Describe your business development strategy for the next five years.

4. What differentiates your organization from competing groups – both in technology and business model or process?

5. Please provide at three least references – including company name, name and title of an executive contact, phone number, and e-mail address – whom we may contact to review projects similar to our application that are in production.

6. Describe projects you have completed that are similar to the effort indicated by this proposal, including:

   a. Number of users
   b. Number of transactions in a day
   c. Hardware, operating systems, and data bases
   d. Length of time it took to build and implement the system
   e. When the project went into production

SECTION SIX

Partnering

"The Teacher is also the Taught."

– Guru Granth Sahib*

A classic Dilbert cartoon shows the downtrodden cubicle inmate saying, "Thank God there are vendors!" Having been in the corner office myself, is it any surprise that I want to be a partner, not a vendor?

RATHER A PARTNER THAN A VENDOR BE

Some IT managers are tempted to ask multiple vendors to compete for each piece of every project of any significance. It is sobering to think of the costs of doing so in an offshore situation.

But don't forget that, unlike office supply vendors, global software teams are unique because of the distance, time zones, and national cultures involved. As Professor Erran Carmel outlined in his book *Global Software Teams[1]*, there are five centrifugal forces potentially tearing these teams apart. According to Carmel, these forces result from geographic dispersion, loss of communication richness, coordination breakdown, loss of "team-ness," and cultural differences.

---

*The Sikh holy scriptures containing the works of its own religious founders and of saints from other faiths. It is revered as The Supreme Spiritual Authority and The Living Guru of the Sikhs.

[1] Publisher – Prentice Hall PTR (1999)

The professor goes on to say that these forces can be managed successfully by the following six "centripetal" forces:

- Telecommunications infrastructure
- Product architecture
- Development methodology
- Collaborative technology
- Managerial technique
- Team building

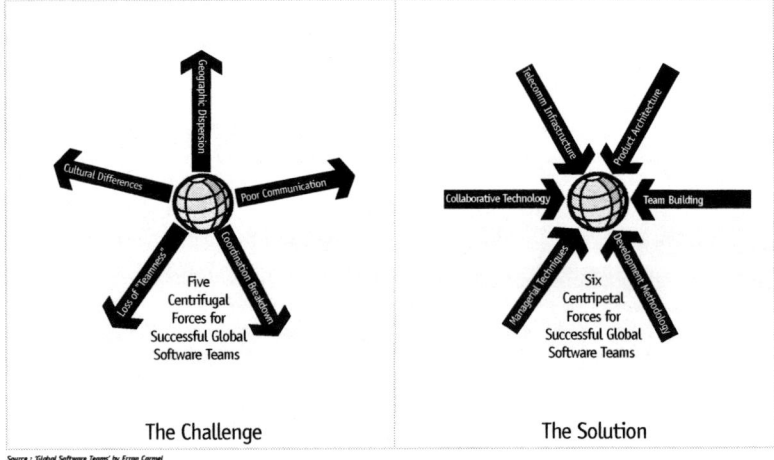

Source : 'Global Software Teams' by Erran Carmel

Graphic #32: The Dynamics of Globally Dispersed Software Development

We covered these forces – both potentially divisive and potentially unifying – elsewhere in this text. It is important to note that these centripetal forces require client and vendor alike invest in a relationship. It simply doesn't come as a standard package "off the shelf." I believe the only reason both buyers and sellers invest in projects of any significance is that both sides have the intention (or there is at least the possibility) to build a true partnership. Clearly, partnerships take time to establish and nurture, so let's begin with the process of going from a "vendorship" to a partnership.

FROM VENDORSHIP TO PARTNERSHIP

There is a continuum of options for the vendor/partner relationship starting with a pure "rental" focus and going all the way to shared or complete ownership. The differences along this continuum are as much attitudinal as contractual.

1. The *rental relationship* is typically a time and materials assignment where the client pays for staff onsite and/or offshore for a defined period.
2. The *fixed bid project* where the relationship is still contractual on a project-by-project basis is a deeper relationship between the corporation and vendor. The buyer orders services or other deliverables based on service levels, with project responsibility transferred to the vendor.
3. The *capacity deal* approaches a partnership orientation and has several shades of control versus price advantages. In these arrangements the buyer contracts for a certain number of resources. These are managed directly by the buyer or by the offshore partner. When the buyer manages the capacity, it is like a committed time and materials deal with the onus for utilization and productivity lying with the buyer. The alternative is to let the offshore provider manage the resources with transparency on utilization and service level agreements.
4. In *partnerships* and *joint ventures* the two parties are committed to common goals, as opposed to purchase agreements. These arrangements may include agreements to share revenues – if both partners jointly serve end customers – or build performance-based compensation plans. A capacity deal is, therefore, the basis, but partnerships go beyond capacity based SLAs to business goals.
5. In an *ownership* situation, the offshore facility is owned directly or indirectly by the corporation.

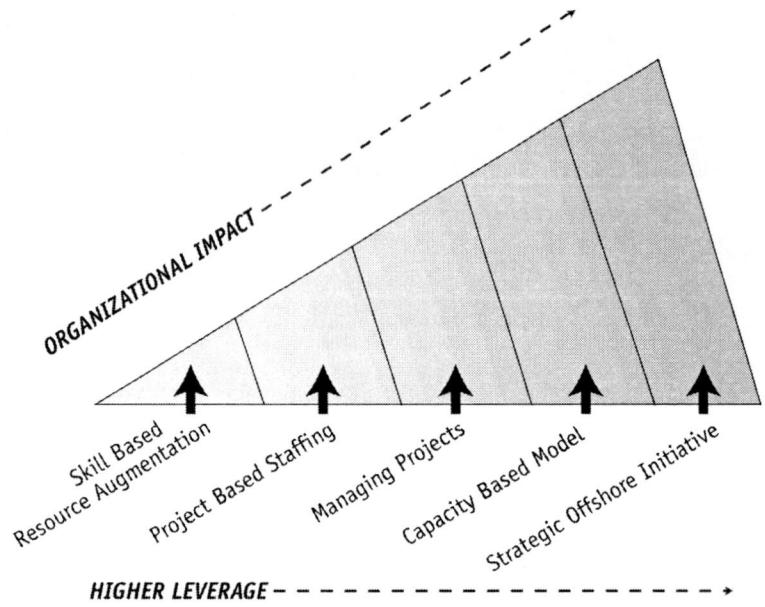

ORGANIZATIONAL IMPACT

Skill Based Resource Augmentation

Project Based Staffing

Managing Projects

Capacity Based Model

Strategic Offshore Initiative

HIGHER LEVERAGE – – – – – – – – – – – – – – – – – – – →

Graphic #33: Vendor to Partner – Greater investment in offshore outsourcing leads to higher leverage of resources and investment

These options balance total cost of ownership, capability building, control, and risk. While the rental option seems the simplest and most efficient – and may well be in the short term – this approach neither builds capability nor the "team-ness" and collaborative approach needed to build a sustained business advantage. In a partnership, the offshore partner is accountable for productivity, utilization, and – jointly with the client – development of offshoring skills in the client organization and domain knowledge in the provider. This leads to a joint ownership of business results.

Majesco manages several outsourcing relationships in which a percentage of earnings is linked to the achievement of the business goals that the IT application supports. This means our company is accountable for business results, rather than mere IT deliverables . . . or worse, a 'black hole.'

This section describes some of the issues related to a vendor-type arrangement. It also describes a preferred virtual joint venture format that is applicable in most situations.

Some of the common issues encountered in working with vendors on a project basis are:

- Cost of bidding
- Knowledge loss
- Master-slave relationship
- Change management overhead

A brief discussion of these issues is important.

COST OF BIDDING

The cost of "relationship hopping" – in life and in business – is seldom well understood. Changing horses is expensive. At a major bank, a 10-person team spent four to six months on an offshore RFP and vendor selection process. That represented nearly five person-years of effort. If that isn't enough expense to make you think twice, the team is often supplemented by expensive consultant firms.

A recent issue of *CIO* magazine took a hard look at the costs of offshoring, estimating that the expense of selecting a service provider can cost from 0.2 percent to 2 percent of the annual cost of the overall project. If you plan to invest $10 million in work offshore, the cost of selecting a vendor would range from $20,000 to $200,000 . . . every time you contemplate a change in vendors.

These selection costs include documenting requirements, sending out RFPs and evaluating the responses, plus negotiating a contract. A project leader may work full time on this effort with others working on various elements, as needed, plus the legal fees. All of this represents added cost. Some companies hire an outsourcing adviser or consultant, adding still more to the overall cost. On top of these out-of-pocket costs, the entire process takes from six months to a year, depending on the nature of the relationship. Expect to spend an additional 1 to 10 percent on vendor selection and initial travel costs.

While some of this is justifiable, at the front end of an offshoring decision it is more difficult to see the logic for even a watered-down version of this process for ongoing project allocation. Processes and committees cannot take the place of management decision-making. As adman David Ogilvy once said, "Scan your parks . . . you will find no statues for committees."

Knowledge Loss

While some costs are a part of doing business offshore, knowledge loss need not be. When vendors and teams change frequently, the knowledge gained from working on one set of assignments is lost. Even within the same vendor, if work is parceled out one project at a time, it is very likely the vendor will be unable to maintain the project team intact. The resulting loss of knowledge and continuity is a huge problem, albeit one whose dollar cost is probably impossible to estimate.

In fact, one key argument often cited for avoiding outsourcing altogether is the need for stability of resources. While offshoring certainly delivers stability, the gains can erode rapidly if clients constantly shop around. A long term partnership with a dedicated vendor is far superior.

Master-Slave Relationship

Customers who often deal with many different vendors typically behave in a certain manner. Whether they like it or not, IT departments must deal with hardware vendors, software vendors, network vendors, ISPs, supplies vendors (for items such as printer paper and cartridges), special products vendors, and many more. They must negotiate the best deals with all vendors, and tend to hold them on a tight leash – whether through SLAs or the threat of moving the business to another vendor. In short, they exercise authoritative power over the vendor. The vendor responds in a Pavlovian manner, trying to please the customer. This is then a master-slave relationship. On the other hand, with a partner, meeting SLAs is a joint responsibility, and hence it is necessary that each side cooperate with the other.

An example from our Asian division illustrates the point. A major Japanese customer sent a project manager to India after signing the contract. On his first day in the office we introduced him to key people in the organization, gave him a series of presentations, treated him to lunch, and finally took him out for dinner that evening.

He did not look happy, so we asked if something was wrong. Speaking frankly, he told us that we were treating him like a customer the whole day. We were taken aback and said that he *was* a customer to us. He replied that it shouldn't work that way . . . that we must work as partners, as equals. We took his comments to heart and, six years later, that relationship continues.

CHANGE MANAGEMENT OVERHEAD

There are some subtle impacts involved with a vendor relationship. The classic vendor relationship mandates that requirements for the new system be laid out very clearly. First, the act of preparing these requirements to the necessary level of detail is difficult and time consuming. Since the process is never perfect, a lot of energy has to go into managing the inevitable stream of change orders that come along during the program.

Secondly, the vendor must build an onerous change management process to document each change for management and technical purposes. In addition, a significant amount of management time must be invested on both sides to create a paper trail and documentation to justify actions within the context of the contract, should it become necessary. Also in a typical client/vendor relationship, the vendor has a vested interest in reducing the overall level of work to manage the profit margin.

When the relationship is elevated to the level of a partnership, on the other hand, nearly all these issues are greatly mitigated. In a partnership, change requests – while still requiring a managed process – are defined in joint working sessions. The nature of the partnership makes costs easier to manage because of the transparency of the relationship.

To realize the full potential savings of offshoring, it is critical that both teams work in harmony as one team with very little overlap. An approach which works well for us is sending a client team member to our center in India to perform testing. An alternative involves having a manager from the client company serve as a communications interface between the two teams. Ideally, the structure allows you to pull resources in

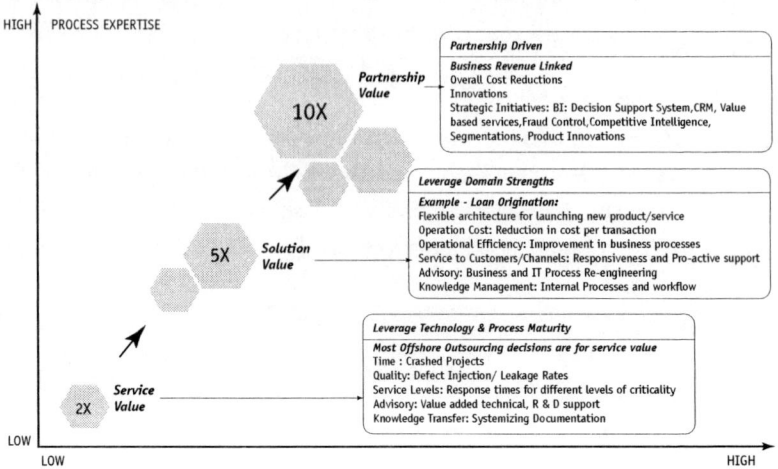

Graphic #34: Moving up the Majesco Value Chain – During the three stages of value generation, returns on investment increase from a factor of 2 to a high of 10 as you get increasingly larger benefits from service, solution and partnership arrangements

from both sides to allocate work based on skills and efficiency, not on which company the person comes from. This model – working collaboratively as one team – provides higher levels of efficiency and productivity than is possible within the context of the typical vendor contract management system.

Vendor Frustrations

The number one frustration all outsourcing vendors share arises when someone with the client company "stonewalls," or insists on clearing every single decision with senior executive management.

One of my mentors, Jerry Rao, presently the chairman of Mphasis, presciently noted that "we'll know the recession has ended when AVPs (assistant vice presidents) can make project decisions again."

Another industry leader, the head of a major U.S. outsourcing company, put it this way: "Even CEOs are sometimes not empowered ... we like it when consultants are involved because they will force a decision."

Our own experience is very similar. Decision making on almost every aspect of some projects is delayed in 40 percent. In some cases, these delays last over six months, and in 20 percent of the cases delays last more than a year. These "beauty contests" involving continuous tendering and delayed decisions impose both real and opportunity costs for everyone involved.

Once you complete a due diligence review prior to beginning the project, I strongly recommend a partnership approach – with two or more vendors if warranted by the magnitude of the effort – that includes periodic external benchmarks to ensure that the relationship isn't being taken for granted.

WHY NOT A CAPTIVE?

Given an elevated understanding of the goals of offshoring, it's important to review some of the other options available – outright ownership or a captive vendor.

A company like HSBC (formerly Hong Kong Banking Corporation) can successfully build a captive facility in India because it has been in

India for 150 years. But most user organizations – and many external service providers, as well – are better off leaving management of technology and operations in India to the companies whose sole business is doing so.

Further, any technology community thrives in its own ecosystem complete with role models, career paths, relatively flat organization and compensation structures, transparency, and peer review processes . . . and above all a near disdain for all that is not technology. This environment is hard to create within a large financial services company or a retailer.

In addition, specialty technology and outsourcing companies maintain support functions that client organizations can leverage. These functions include solution architects, who can work with business analysts to develop pilots and prototypes, research cells able to work on identifying new technologies and benchmarking existing, versus new, processes, plus consultants who can help ensure quality and process rigor.

The CEO of a top 12 bank sums up the choice as being between 'heavy chaperone' or 'light chaperone' . . . but never 'no chaperone' or going it alone. This CEO understands that building and managing a captive vendor in India is anything but a trivial exercise. The decision should not be taken lightly.

THE VJV – JOINED AT THE HIP

The preferred business model is a partnership model with common goals. For partnership arrangements there are three broad options:

- No ownership
- Part ownership
- Full ownership

The classic joint venture structures are well known. One alternative that needs to be considered is a virtual joint venture (VJV). I believe the VJV will gain popularity quickly since it allows for independence and focus, as is the case in a classic JV, while avoiding the potential legal quagmire that can accompany the formation of a company.

Here are some thoughts on the structure and governing principles.

These thoughts assume a critical mass of a unit with a staff of at least 100, with the potential to grow to times that number. The central idea of dedicated center(s) and accountability can be adapted for smaller units.

The VJV runs like an independent Strategic Business Unit – with its own strategic and tactical plan, staff, and P&L. This "virtual" joint venture avoids the legal and financial overhead of a separate organization. The VJV must have a full-time CEO with accountability for the entity's business goals. Accountability moves from Service Level Agreements to monetary value.

The CEO of the VJV entity reports to a governing board with senior representation from both organizations, including business line executives. This board plays an active role in defining the strategy of the entity and ensuring that both companies' resources are available to the entity.

The VJV needs a dedicated Offshore Development Center head in India to coordinate activities on behalf of the entity in India. Initially, the VJV draws on resources from the Indian partner. Later, the entity can maintain its own bench from offshore to ensure knowledge retention. Corporate functions and services – human resources, finance, and information technology including the software process group and solution architecture groups – from both companies support the VJV structure, as needed.

SHARING THE SPOILS

Financial arrangements between the client and outsourcing partner need to facilitate the following:

- Distribution of rewards must be fair and equitable, based on the value added by the parties.
- Arrangements must be sustainable for the long run and encourage performance by the parties. (Performance-based compensation works well. This links the delivery of technology and operational services to the achievement of business results.)
- It's important to strike a balance between the short-term and long-term financial goals of both partners. (You may need to

trade off immediate savings to gain the longer-term benefits of building a bench, competency, and infrastructure.)

- Collective management of risk as perceived by both parties is important. (This includes the risk of disasters, skill availability, bench strength, and people. Also, transparency and shared objectives reduce risks overall and make the proposition even more attractive to both parties.)
- The potential for equity upside is significant if the buyer wishes to participate in this high growth sector.
- Many offshore firms trade at higher multiples than their buyer partners. It may be attractive for the client company to use some of its profits to buy equity in the supplier firm. This arrangement can provide many of the advantages of building your own supplier without the effort and hassles involved. But, as with any equity investment, caveat emptor applies. Most Indian firms are U.S. GAAP compliant. However, most are small to mid-sized companies with respect to capitalization – from $50 million to $500 million – with correspondingly lower liquidity.

Building a level of ownership through a build-operate-transfer arrangement is certainly an option some clients may want to consider. This approach can offer greater control over the venture. It also offers the possibility of spinning-off the venture eventually.

However, while such an equity-based option may be appropriate in some situations, it is probably not worth exercising in most cases. Many of the desired gains can be realized through the VJV.

MUTUAL MASTERY

Partnerships, in whatever form, ultimately make the client firm more competitive than the traditional client/vendor relationship. If speed is the defining differentiator for our age, then clearly an offshore partnership allows greater flexibility to expand (or contract), while retaining learning and keeping up with the latest advances. Experience shows that once American project managers, domain experts, and programmers travel to India – with all their mental reservations and preconceptions – they experience first-hand the obvious advantages of the onsite-offshore model. They see the benefits of time-zone difference and realize that cultural differences are not so difficult. They become converts.

Like a mystical moment that can only be experienced, but not explained, PowerPoint presentations and white papers on the subject of offshoring and partnering only do so much. What invariably works is a visit to India by the American customer or prospect.

At the same time, Indians who become "Americanized" find the process is remarkably easy because Americans are the friendliest, most accepting people anywhere in the world.

Smart developers and project leaders apply their intelligence and work ethic to learning the client's business and integrating themselves culturally. Thus, both buyer and seller simultaneously become more independent and dependent on each other. In the end state, the buyer is leveraging offshore directly with few partner resources – in effect he/she is a master and offshore providers can be a "fungible commodity."

At the same time, the technical professionals from India travel and learn their client's business and can move on to build other vertical relationships. It is at this stage of freedom that the truly symbiotic partnership flourishes and produces extraordinary results.

SECTION SEVEN

MAINTAINING QUALITY . . .
AND USER SATISFACTION

"Learning is not compulsory . . . neither is survival."
—W. Edwards Deming*

THE TOTAL QUALITY REVOLUTION

The quality movement, or Total Quality Management (TQM) as it is popularly referred to, grew out of the work of Dr. W. Edwards Deming. Deming was largely responsible for the quality revolution in Japan. Japan was the first country to recognize the far-reaching implications of TQM. Their early adoption of Deming's methods had a huge impact on the competitiveness of Japanese products, especially automobiles.

Prior to the advent of TQM, the standard approach to quality entailed inspecting products as they rolled off the assembly line, rejecting any faulty items, and sending the rejects back for rework. This approach ensured that any faulty product that was identified was fixed, but did nothing to get at the cause of error. When your car has a problem, you get it fixed, but in most cases, information about the problem ends in the

*Out of the Crisis, Publisher – SPC Press (February 1982)

173

dealer's shop. This is a very expensive way to operate, since the cost of a dealer repair is far greater than the cost of doing it right the first time.

Deming taught that the basis for achieving Total Quality was a never-ending effort to find and remove each production process that caused an error. Fixing each defective product was much less important than going through the arduous task of finding why the defect occurred in the first place. This required a total change in how the organization operated.

 # DEMING'S 14 POINTS

1. Create constancy of purpose towards improvement.
2. Adopt a new philosophy (toward poor quality).
3. Cease dependence on mass inspection. Require statistical evidence.
4. End the practice of awarding business based on price.
5. Find problems. It's management's job to always work on the system.
6. Institute modern methods of training on the job.
7. Institute modern methods of supervision (change from numbers to quality).
8. Drive out fear.
9. Break down barriers between departments.
10. Eliminate numerical goals and slogans that ask for new levels of productivity without providing methods.
11. Eliminate work standards that prescribe numerical quotas.
12. Remove barriers that stand between the hourly worker and his right to pride of workmanship.
13. Institute a vigorous program of education and retraining.
14. Top management commitment to other 13 points everyday.

Graphic #35: Deming's 14 Points

The table shown above of Deming's fabled "14 Points" shows just how far reaching changes in an organization need to be to achieve Total Quality.

Every employee in an organization must be completely dedicated to the task of finding and eliminating the root causes of defects – the errors in the process itself. Deming also taught that, in order for TQM to work, detailed measurements are required. The fight for quality is fought statistically over all the elements involved in the production process, not at the individual event level. The TQM effort is directed at grinding down the statistics by a series of continual changes. Achieving quality takes time and total dedication.

THE PROMISE OF TQM

Often, the first reaction to TQM is the assumption that it will cost a lot of money. Implementing TQM requires investment, but the very significant savings that result more than offset the initial costs. The later in the production process an error is detected, the more expensive it is to fix. Consider how expensive it is to fix a problem after you receive your car, not to mention the impact on the company's reputation. A significant part of every company's cost base is defect repair.

TQM drives defect repair costs down as far as possible. Not only does this reduce costs overall, but it is also an important market differentiator. Experience at many companies that have adopted TQM bear this out.

There are several different systems being deployed to achieve high quality. They include:

- The original Deming TQM system set forth in his books and papers,
- The 6-Sigma program originated by Motorola, and
- The International Specification Organization's ISO-9000.

Each of these programs is different from the others, but all aim at the same goal – achieving the highest possible quality in business processes.

TQM AND SOFTWARE OUTSOURCING
EARLY SOFTWARE MANAGEMENT

As TQM gathered momentum in hardware manufacturing, a number of groups began thinking about applying the same methodologies to software development. But, don't assume this is a straightforward application. For many years, people viewed software development as more of an art than a science. Typically, software development was viewed as a brilliant programmer working independently to create exciting new applications.

The more complex software projects became, however, they required the work teams of programmers producing different elements that were then integrated into a larger system. Several different management techniques sprang to life, all trying to get some clear management discipline into the process.

Many different methods were tried. Despite the best efforts of software managers, software developed a reputation for costing twice what was budgeted, or more, and never being delivered on time. There were exceptions, of course, but the exceptional program that was delivered on time usually came at high cost.

ENTER CARNEGIE-MELLON

Eventually, the computer sciences department at Carnegie Mellon University developed a new approach to software development and quality. Known as the Carnegie Mellon Maturity Model, they developed a 5 phase process to go from a development model that was essentially in chaos to one that was tightly managed and readily measured. Software development organizations that achieved the top level are popularly referred to as CMM-5.

Watts Humphrey and a team of researchers in the Software Engineering Institute at Carnegie Mellon University originally developed the CMM model as part of a project funded by the U.S. Air Force. The objective of this effort was a method to evaluate the effectiveness of software contractors. As part of this study, researchers analyzed the strengths and weaknesses of the organizations that they evaluated to find which characteristics best determined an organization's capabilities.

Researchers discovered that the maturity of an organization's processes was directly related to its performance. As expected, those organizations that follow formal, well-defined processes are far more effective than "ad hoc" organizations. Further, they found that organizations could be arranged into well-defined categories based upon their level of process maturity. These categories became the levels of the CMM.

Although the model originally was built to evaluate software contractors, its value to IS organizations was quickly recognized. In addition to providing a framework for analyzing organizational maturity, the model provides a road map for progressing to higher levels of maturity.

The Capability Maturity Model provides a template for evaluating the process maturity of an organization by comparing that organization against a series of well-defined levels. Each level is a plateau on the path toward becoming a mature software organization. The characteristics of each level are easily described, as is the set of actions required to reach the subsequent level. The model formalizes the process of determining organizational maturity and provides a road map for improvement.

After introducing the model, Carnegie Mellon developed a measurement process which allowed a trained evaluator to place a software organization into one of the five levels. It is important to note that this evaluation process involves as much art as science. While not exact, the process looks at the major features of the software management system in use.

What is CMM-5 Anyway?

Our real interest is in understanding the characteristics of a CMM-5 shop. It's useful to think back to the hardware process analogy. In a CMM-1 or CMM-2 organization, the focus is entirely on finding and fixing errors.

At the other end of the spectrum is a CMM-5 organization, which looks for the root cause of every error to implement corrections as early in the process as possible, just as in the hardware case. Also, as in the hardware case, every aspect of the software development process is measured including programmer productivity, keeping on schedule, error rates, etc.

As was pointed out earlier, reaching this level of performance requires significant amounts of training and the complete buy-in of the staff. For this reason, it can be a lengthy and expensive process. In some cases, it is impractical for corporate software departments to develop a CMM-5 rating.

In India, many outsourcing companies have invested heavily in reaching level CMM-5. As discussed earlier, fully 50 of the 74 companies assessed at Level 5 worldwide are in India! It is important to note that with fixed price contracting, an outsourcing company lives or dies by its ability to meet cost and schedule goals. This is in contrast to many internal IT organizations, where software development is just one of many activities. For an outsourcer, it is their only business and they devote all of their management efforts to building the quality of their delivered product.

THE CMM MODEL AND ITS LEVELS

The best method for understanding the value of the CMM is to understand each level of the model and its characteristics. The model defines five distinct stages of increasing process maturity:

- Initial
- Repeatable
- Defined
- Managed
- Optimized

As organizations move up the ladder from level to level, productivity is enhanced and risk is minimized. The following summaries describe the basic characteristics of each level of the CMM model, showing the progression to a carefully managed environment – CMM-5.

LEVEL 1 : COME IN AND PROGRAM

Chief Characteristics

- Visibility into progress is limited
- Long working hours
- Work pressure builds closer to delivery date
- Quality is based on how much one can test
- Generally tends to have a lot of rework
- Success depends on heroes in the team

Organizations at this level are known as "**Chaotic**." At this level, software delivery success rests on the individual. If the individual is organized and manages all parts of the software delivery process, then there is a reasonable possibility of meeting the Scope, Time, and Quality (STQ) requirements of an engagement.

Typically, these organizations lack formalized procedures for most of their work areas. If any formal procedure exists, it lacks the management mechanism required to ensure organization wide usage. Software professionals in these organizations tend to view quality assurance efforts as unnecessary overhead not directly related to delivery of their work efforts. They typically fail to understand the consequences of their "chaotic" behavior. There is very little formalization of process, and hence successes are difficult to repeat and failures difficult to avoid. You find most individual "heroes" in Level 1 Organizations.

Normally, software organizations at this level are vulnerable, and their operations are not scaleable.

LEVEL 2: PLAN WHAT YOU'RE DOING

Chief Characteristics

- Requirements and resources are known
- A minimum plan (Work Breakdown Structure) to meet the requirement is in place
- Delivery and quality of work products ensured through reviews and audits
- Review mechanism of sub contractors' delivery is in place
- Basic discipline of configuration control is observed
- Greater focus on control

Organizations at this level rely heavily on rigorous project management to control their efforts and meet project, cost, and time commitments. Although these enhancements are rudimentary from a process perspective, they can accomplish dramatic improvements in operational performance over Level 1 organizations. Although Level 2 organizations have formal planning and project controls in place, the bulk of their procedures are institutionalized through staff experience rather than documentation. This greatly increases the difficulty of adapting to new situations.

Essentially, organizations at this level are **"Reactive."** Level 2 organizations focus on managing the project requirements, detailing the requirements to WBS, controlling the configuration, verifying the activities performed through SQAs, and monitoring regularly to see that everything proceeds according to plan. These controls allow the organization to successfully repeat previously mastered tasks and avoid the repetition of failures.

Organizations at this level have yet to learn to leverage the best practices from one engagement to successfully carry out another.

LEVEL 3: GET SERIOUS ABOUT PROJECT MANAGEMENT

Chief Characteristics

Typical characteristics of a Level 3 organization are that it:

· Establishes a responsibility center which defines and institutionalizes processes
· Establishes an organizational process database
· Learns from other projects and makes this information available throughout the organization
· Provides multiple choices for executing engagements
· Selects and applies the best, most suitable engineering practices
· Based on the organization database, establishes an integrated approach to executing and managing the engagement
· Establishes clear definitions of responsibilities for all groups contributing to the success of engagement and gains their complete commitment

At this level, processes are not only formally defined and documented, but are well understood and followed. These organizations essentially behave in a "**Proactive**" fashion. A dedicated group – the software engineering process group (SEPG) – is established to manage the Organizational Process Database, which includes a quality management system, information on lessons learned from past engagements, standards, etc.

The organization database is the foundation for plans for any new project. As a result, everyone implements the same task in the same manner. New processes and tools are introduced with minimal disruption to the work effort. Training enables new staff members to adopt the organization's practices easily.

A Level 3 organization's plan is not merely a WBS. In addition to an estimated WBS, Level 3 organizations address other aspects of the project engagement including:

- What is the customer's expectation?
- What processes – management and software engineering – do we follow to achieve this goal?
- Have we involved all the concerned parties?
- Do we understand the risk factors and have appropriate mitigation plans?

In a Level 3 organization, considerable emphasis is placed on achieving results through peer review, which improves both the possibility of finding defects as well as educating all peers on the software.

Organizations at this level leverage the benefits gained from past projects effectively and are normally stable and uniform in their delivery practices.

LEVEL 4: MEASURE AND PREDICT

Chief Characteristics

- Explicitly address the customer's needs as part of a philosophy of quality management
- The production of the software product is quantitatively understood throughout the software process
- Applies the principles of statistical process control, addressing

special causes of process variation
- Fixes problems in the process itself

Organizations at this level learn to be "**Predictive**." The Project Plan – designed to meet customer expectations – outlines aspects needed to execute the project execution. But how do we know that the customer's expectations are met? How do we know that expectations have not changed? How can we predict we can meet these expectations based on the capability of the team or the organization? How do we know that the processes followed are effective and efficient? The Level 4 organization brings in the discipline of quantitatively defining these measures, analyzing them, adjusting the tools and processes appropriately, and predicting the capability to deliver.

Organizations at this level know what commitments they can make based on their capability and predict the delivery against STQ.

LEVEL 5: THE WHOLE ENCHILADA

Chief Characteristics

- Major contributors to defects are known and plans are in place to prevent them from recurring
- Promotes a culture of individuals committed to preventing defects
- Automate, pilot new technologies, do technology transition
- Identifies and eliminates chronic causes of poor performances
- Continually improves the software process
- Process improvement becomes a way of life

Level 5 is all about "**Optimizing**." At Level 4 one is able to predict the number of defects that would be injected at each phase, how many of those would get detected, and therefore judge the effectiveness of development processes. At Level 5, the organization plans how to prevent defects from happening in the first place, optimizing the performance of the processes.

In addition, at this level the organization starts soliciting process improvements at the organizational level. At Level 5, processes are not changed to suit an individual's convenience. Rather, processes are changed to achieve better results and to deliver better value to all the stakeholders.

The accompanying diagram depicts the benefits of a properly implemented CMM model in a simple yet powerful manner. As you go up the levels you find that the **time and quality** aspects of delivery **improve** and there is an increasing **probability** that the results will match the original plan.

Level	Process Characteristics	Predicted Performance
5 **Optimizing**	Process improvement is institutionalized.	*(graph: Probability vs Time / $ / Quality, Target N-z)*
4 **Managed**	Product and processes are quantitatively controlled.	*(graph: Probability vs Time / $ / Quality, Target N-y)*
3 **Defined**	Technically practices are integrated with management practices and institutionalized.	*(graph: Probability vs Time / $ / Quality, Target N-y)*
2 **Repeatable**	Project management practices are institutionalized.	*(graph: Probability vs Time / $ / Quality, Target N-y)*
1 **Initial**	Process is informal and ad hoc.	*(graph: Probability vs Time / $ / Quality, Target N-y)*

Graphic #36: The Five Levels of CMM – Better quality through better process

How Does a CMM-5 Organization Operate?

Companies that achieve CMM Level 5 are mature organizations that work proactively to preempt the occurrence of errors. Continuous process improvement strategies are built into software development practices to ensure that customer expectations are met for each and every delivery cycle.

These practices are nothing but standard and consistent methods to review, monitor, and optimize the project processes to achieve high value delivery. This level of quality is embedded in the organization's software development processes. Product and process quality are highly predictable in nature. The delivery model defines quality up front and acquaints the customer with the processes that deal with monitoring and measuring the quality of deliverables continuously.

Furthermore, people are empowered and committed to meeting the customer's expectations. In summary, a CMM Level 5 organization's focus is on:

- Improved productivity – for both internal and external deliverables
- Better predictability and lower risks during the project
- Improved product quality
- Proven processes resulting in shortened time-to-market
- Increased adaptability to change
- Access to a global pool of the industry's best talent

The Importance of Measurement

Measurements are carried out on both the developed product as well as the process. Product metrics are defined and measured to manage the development and delivery of the product while process metrics are defined and measured to determine the implementation of the development and delivery process.

Metrics used for measurement include:

- Efficiency
- Scope
- Defect leakage to onsite
- Predictability of on-time delivery

How Are the Measurements Used?

The measurements are key elements in setting project goals, conducting process and product progress reviews, taking corrective action and making continuous improvements, and for monitoring organizational processes. The specific manners in which these are used are outlined below.

Project goal setting

Project team members sign up for the requisite product quality and process compliance by setting project goals at the start of the project. These goal-setting parameters – Quality Utilisation, Estimation, Scope and Timeliness (QUEST) – are identified as performance indicators to measure the project progress on a continuous basis.

Process and product progress reviews

- A project management tool captures project data. This is used as the standard tool throughout the organization and acts as a common repository for process data. The tool also helps review process for continuous process improvements.
- The Software Quality Assurance, Project Managers, and Delivery Heads continuously monitor project progress and process compliance. Product and process quality is reviewed at every stage of development.
- The Defect Management process identifies the sources and causes of the defects, prioritizes and systematically removes them, and upgrades the defect prevention measures so that the defects do not recur during development.
- The verification and validation process ensures that product quality problems are detected early in the development and do not impact the quality of delivery, scope of the project, timeliness of the delivery, or the efficiency of resources. Project scorecards and defect logs are central elements in project reviews.

Corrective action and continuous improvements

Consolidated non-compliances, issues, and project related risk areas are reported to projects. Senior management participates in reviews of the overall project status on a regular basis. Action plans are defined based on these inputs, and then implemented.

Organization process measurements

· Whenever a project team experiences problems in any areas, it always informs the quality group about the root causes of such problems and the possible solutions. Process data analysis removes common causes of organization process variations. Such analysis also works to improve overall process stability.

· Customer survey feedbacks, suggestions from team members, and strategic input from management provide key feedback for organization process improvement.

Measurement Examples

The chart below gives an idea of the kind of measurements that are used in the organization.

No.	Measurements	Description
1	Leakage to customer	Numbers of defects detected at onsite / Total number of defects found in the projects
2	Program Specification Defect Injection rate (DIR of Specs)	Number of defects identified Specs as source / Total defects found in the project
3	Code Defect Injection rate (DIR of Code)	Number of defects identified Code as source / Total defects found in the project
4	Code Defect Detection rate (DDR of Code)	Number of defects detected at Specs phase / Total defects found in the project
5	Code Review Effectiveness	Number of defects expected in the code phase / Number of defects found in the code phase
6	Efficiency of the project	Efforts planned for development / Actual efforts spent on development

Graphic #37: Quality Measurement Examples

Customer Reporting

Customer reporting is an invaluable mechanism to gather feedback from the customer and use it to further improve the quality process. In the typical CMM Level 5 organizations:

- Customer feedback is one of the chief measures of quality of delivery and quality of process in the project.
- Gathering customer feedback through customer survey occurs on a regular basis.
- All customer complaints regarding a project deliverable are addressed and closed by the respective project team.
- The quality department maintains a record of customer complaints to identify problem areas in the process. Solutions for such problem areas are then developed and incorporated in the process through an improvement action plan.
- Client Feedback Analysis helps identify problems and set priorities on those improvements that are most meaningful to the client.

Continuous Feedback

Continuous feedback is an equally valued process and is used rigorously to enhance quality levels. In the representative CMM Level 5 company, continuous feedback and process improvement initiatives are regularly planned throughout the organization level and appropriate actions are implemented as per plan. Typically, the process followed aims to:

- Assess the current situation on the basis of QUEST performance
- List and prioritize areas for improvement
- Prepare an action plan for the identified areas
- Implement action plan through the active participation of team members
- Verify the effectiveness of the implementation through regular process and management reviews

Generally speaking, a top-down approach is taken to align processes with the strategic plan. A bottom-up approach is, however, used for process inconsistencies or suggestions reported by team members that are used as inputs to refine processes. Such an approach has the added advantage of fostering a culture where team members can and do make suggestions on the fly.

Every project team maintains process databases, audit non-compliance reports, and deviation requests. These constitute a repository of shared knowledge that is used to identify improvement areas. The project manager and software quality assurance ensure that the development process is periodically assessed and evaluated for process improvements. The SQA also conducts a periodic audit to ensure the effectiveness of continuous improvement initiatives in the project.

PERFORMANCE ASSESSMENT

Performance is usually assessed at two levels, first at an organization level and second at the project level.

Organization process implementation performance

The quality group facilitates the measurement and analysis of process implementation in several ways, including:

- Identifying relevant changes needed in the existing process
- Reformulating the procedures, if required
- Defining a new procedure or deleting an existing procedure, if required
- Taking appropriate action

Project process implementation performance:

While assessing project level implementation performance

- A metrics collection and analysis process is defined to help project teams understand the product quality and software development process performance. The metrics collected are identified on the basis of project objectives, product quality and customer satisfaction.

· Project score cards and defects logs along with Statistical Process Control (SPC) techniques like control charts, fish bone diagram, scatter diagram, and run charts are used to monitor product and process effectiveness.

Quality personnel assigned to the project and the project managers ensure that the metrics collected are reviewed regularly. Results of metrics analysis are used as the basis for corrective and preventive actions and for identifying process improvements.

Indian CMM Level 5 software services companies have spent significant time and resources perfecting their development processes and methodologies. As a result, American and European companies can sleep well at night knowing that the work going on in India will be performed with the highest levels of discipline and will be readily measurable.

But don't worry, your own organization need not be certified at CMM Level 5. As long as your partner is.

SECTION EIGHT

MUSINGS ABOUT THE FUTURE

"Growth for the West depends on growth in the East."
—Sudhakar Ram, CEO, Mastek

Congratulations and thank you. By reading this book to this final section, you have demonstrated that you believe, or at least are intrigued, by offshoring, which really opens the door (wider, where it is already open) to globality. And thanks for bearing with me for nearly 200 pages . . . I ask for another five to share a few personal observations about the future.

I hope, maybe even expect, that anyone who has read this book cover to cover is now thinking seriously about globality. Globality is not a place or a process. It is a state of mind. Globally oriented people have the humility, confidence, and vision to understand that the best methodology, the best products and the best services may not always be in their immediate surroundings. Even the mighty Microsoft with 50,000 of the world's best programmers doesn't think that the world stops at Redmond's doors. After all, there are 12 million programmers worldwide. In fact, Bill Gates has said that outsourcing mission-critical work offshore is now "a common-sense proposition."

I have been fortunate to grow with global influences. I attended an Irish missionary school, a liberal arts college set up by the British (complete with a PG Wodehouse society!), a business school affiliated with Harvard, worked at global companies like Cheeseborough Ponds, American Express, Citigroup and now Mastek/Majesco. I have lived in four countries and traveled to over 50. I often think of myself as a modern day gypsy . . . and like the original Romanis (the correct term for 'gypsies,' who interestingly may have originated in India) I really had no choice. My local institutions did not have the same opportunities as those in America.

California is the world's 5th largest economy in a country where opportunities abound. And Americans can fly for hours and still land in an American city. It takes a greater effort for Americans to prepare themselves for a global career. It requires a study of other cultures, history and politics, and not just European countries, but the emerging nations of Asia, South America and Africa, where the greatest opportunities lie. And these foreign cultures are everywhere . . . if we choose to see a foreign film instead of the latest Hollywood release. When we take a date to dine at a Lebanese restaurant or have ale with the guys from work at an Irish pub. Being global is a whole new attitude that will pay off in droves.

The global payoff is on both the revenue and expense lines of a company's income statement. Global expansion of products and markets is a revenue item while global sourcing of IT and ITES is an expense item. And often what starts as an expense save can lead to revenue growth as well. For example, if a bank wants to investigate consumer complaints at an offshore site, the bank has the potential not only to reduce costs and increase revenues. It can also save from $50 to $10 in checking the item. But understand that banks do not check many complaints and just write off most complaints under $100 because they are too small. If that threshold can be lowered from $100 per item to below $50 by offshoring the work, the bank can investigate a larger number of complaints and collect a large number of additional funds.

I daresay I know a key bias that is perhaps holding people back. The bias is that building revenues overseas is better than buying from 'them.'

It is great to see the excitement – the high fives around the office – when a U.S. company acquires a non-U.S. company or launches a new global brand. It worries me when the same people lament when a foreign company succeeds in America or wins a large outsourcing contract.

But you ask: "How can I be a patriotic American and send jobs offshore?"

When I hear that question from business associates or journalists, my answer is that good business requires difficult tradeoffs. Job loss is a real issue, but it has been part of many critical steps in the evolution of our current business environment. Matt Richey, a senior investment analyst who writes for *The Motley Fool*[1] says, "That lost jobs, through productivity gains, can result in higher long-run employment is one of the fundamentally misunderstood paradoxes of economics. The misunderstanding dates back to the Industrial Revolution when English stocking knitters rioted upon introduction of the new stocking frame machinery that made obsolete their manual labor. If only those rioters had realized that within a century, employment in the stocking industry would expand by one hundred fold . . . Corporate America's hiring foray into India will ultimately have the same impact: higher U.S. employment. Yes, there will be dislocated American professionals in the short-run, and their needs should be tended to. But the answer isn't a government blockade against hiring in India."

And Richey continues: "It would be the height of short-sighted folly to think of India's low-cost service sector as anything but a blessing. Out of the increased profits that result, American companies will have the resources to expand elsewhere and thereby create more U.S. jobs."

Other analysts echo these sentiments with the consensus that while churn should be expected, net job loss is less likely.

And, therefore, American companies must stop debating whether to offshore but work instead on how best to do so. In the 1980s, doomsayers shouted from the rooftops that America was being sold off piece by piece to the wily Japanese. America did not become Japan, Inc. then. Nor will we become India, Inc. now. On the contrary, the growing business relationships between my two countries (India and America) will generate job growth in both, India *and* America. Indian companies will succeed only when they Americanize their front end, not just by a token presence in the sales force, but in project managers and developers on-site. The markets and the regulators will force that. To go up in the value chain, it

---

[1] India's Blessed Labor, Motley Fool – August 5, 2003

will become critical to have a better understanding of the local context, and work permit limits will force the pace.

For both American and Indian companies and policy makers the future depends on smart people staying competitive by letting the free markets guide them to the best cost/quality of resources and new markets. What the world needs is trade, not government aid. And, we need free trade in goods, *and* services.

Some final thoughts . . .

Offshoring is part art and part science. I conceived and wrote this book to provide you with a guide through this fundamental economic trend that is offshoring in the Indian context. You will need to learn the business and you probably will want to rely on professional managers and consultants to help speed you along the learning curve. But remember that ethnic backgrounds are not a good substitute for management experience. That idea went out with old school ties.

The pace will quicken. I believe you will find yourself running faster than you ever imagined possible and in directions you never dreamed before. Your customers, competitors and hostile investors will push you. Today outsourcing offshore has become mainstream in the media's consciousness. But in reality, it is not yet mainstream in practice. The offshore movement, per se, is still in the early adopters/visionary phase. In Geoffrey Moore's (*Bridging the Chasm*) terms, we have not yet crossed the chasm, but we are on the verge. The visionaries, the early adopters have made a huge splash. But most agree that the tidal wave of pragmatists or deep-enders is yet to come.

Offshoring will no longer be a Fortune 500 phenomenon. It will be embraced by mid-sized companies across America seeking a competitive advantage. Therefore, the time to get started is *now*.

Not all will go well. While looking for the pot of gold, watch out for fool's gold. The trials will come from within and without. Some will be harder than others. But in the long run the benefits will far outweigh the costs.

Change is the only constant. I see our industry changing. The need for domain knowledge will drive partnerships. The need for scale (as a surrogate for stability) will drive consolidation. The need for more business functions to become offshorable (e.g., call centers, business processing vendors) will drive diversification into IT enabled services. The need for utility-like models will drive complete outsourcing. All of these changes will alter the nature of firms in the industry, but not the basic value proposition. Strong partnerships will create the flexibility needed to take advantage of opportunities as they arise.

India and America – the world's most populous democracies – surprisingly have a shared heritage. And their destinies are becoming more intertwined. Remember Christopher Columbus started out looking for India when he arrived in America. Both countries embraced democracy ahead of capitalism; both are melting pots with a smorgasbord of cultures; both are the leading English-speaking markets, and both produce the most scientists and engineers. GDP projections show America, China and India as the world's largest economies in the future. But America and India have the most in common.

The opportunity for you, gentle reader, is to define your world in the global context. Like Alexander the Great 2,500 years ago, discover India and then build a truly global enterprise. Leverage the resources offshore while building a two-way flow of cultures and best practices. Interestingly, in doing so not only did Alexander and the Hellenic influence grow immeasurably, but he also created opportunities for all who followed him. Thus, as you legitimately ponder the WIIFME issue (What's-In-It-For-ME?); consider this:

Offshoring can create unprecedented opportunities for personal growth and a global legacy for you and your company.

Recommended Additional Reading/Viewing

Books

1. Global Software Teams: Collaborating Across Border and Time Zones – *Erran Carmel, Prentice Hall PTR, 1999* (Organizing and managing cross-border software development teams)
2. India Unbound – *Gurcharan Das, Knopf, 2001* (Indian socio-economic history for the business person)
3. Re-imagine! – *Tom Peters, DK Publishing, 2003* (The shape of things to come; business trends)
4. No Full Stops in India – *Mark Tully, Viking Press, 1999* (Contemporary Indian socio-political history)
5. The Lexus and the Olive Tree – *Tom Friedman, Farrar Straus & Giroux, 2000* (Globalization)
6. The Namesake – *Jhumpa Lahiri, Houghton Mifflin Co, 2003* (Indian immigrant's search for identity in the U.S.)

DVD/Video

1. Monsoon Wedding – *Mira Nair, Universal Studios, 2003* (Indian middle class society)
2. Spellbound – *Jeffrey Blitz, Columbia Tristar, 2004* (High achieving Indian and other schoolchildren)
3. Bend It Like Beckham – *Gurinder Chadha, Twentieth Century Fox, 2003* (Indian immigrant experience in the UK)